Attaching Through Love, Hugs and Play

WITHDRAWN

by the same author

Attaching in Adoption
Practical Tools for Today's Parents
ISBN 978 1 84905 890 2
eISBN 978 0 85700 606 6

Nurturing Adoptions
Creating Resilience after Neglect and Trauma
ISBN 978 1 84905 891 9
eISBN 978 0 85700 607 3

of related interest

Attachment in Common Sense and Doodles
A Practical Guide
Miriam Silver
Foreword by Camila Batmanghelidjh
ISBN 978 1 84905 314 3
eISBN 978 0 85700 624 0

A Short Introduction to Attachment and Attachment Disorder
Colby Pearce
ISBN 978 1 84310 957 0
eISBN 978 1 84642 949 1
Part of the JKP Short Introductions series

Reparenting the Child Who Hurts
A Guide to Healing Developmental Trauma and Attachments
Caroline Archer and Christine Gordon
Foreword by Gregory C. Keck, PhD
ISBN 978 1 84905 263 4
eISBN 978 0 85700 568 7

Why Can't My Child Behave?
Empathic Parenting Strategies that Work for Adoptive and Foster Families
Amber Elliott
Foreword by Kim S. Golding
ISBN 978 1 84905 339 6
eISBN 978 0 85700 671 4

Adopted Like Me
My Book of Adopted Heroes
Ann Angel
Illustrated by Marc Thomas
ISBN 978 1 84905 935 0
eISBN 978 0 85700 740 7

Attaching THROUGH
Love, Hugs AND Play

Simple Strategies to Help Build Connections with Your Child

Deborah D. Gray

Jessica Kingsley *Publishers*
London and Philadelphia

First published in 2014
by Jessica Kingsley Publishers
73 Collier Street
London N1 9BE, UK
and
400 Market Street, Suite 400
Philadelphia, PA 19106, USA

www.jkp.com

Library of Congress Cataloging in Publication Data
Gray, Deborah D., 1951-
  Attaching through love, hugs and play : simple strategies
to help build connections with your child /
Deborah D. Gray.
    pages cm
  ISBN 978-1-84905-939-8
  1. Attachment behavior in children. 2. Parent and child. I. Title.
  BF723.A75G73 2014
  649'.1--dc23
                              2013047022

British Library Cataloguing in Publication Data
A CIP catalogue record for this book is available from the British Library

ISBN 978 1 84905 939 8
eISBN 978 0 85700 753 7

Printed and bound in Great Britain by Bell & Bain Ltd, Glasgow

To Gerald, Patricia, and Summerlea

CONTENTS

ACKNOWLEDGEMENTS

Joe MacKenzie first came up with the concept for this book. He discussed the value of a book with photos—and then agreed to take them. This book was his brain child.

I am grateful for a family and community that provide encouragement to write a book like this. They help me believe in the value of close relationships. Thank you to Colleen Gray, Patricia Gray, Summerlea Gray, Gerald MacKenzie, Joseph MacKenzie Sr., Martha Torlai Mackenzie, and Tricia Mackenzie for your love and allowances, as you made space in your lives for this book.

Thank you to my colleagues and friends who value developing the literature and support for families with attachment challenges: Kristie Baber, Gusty-Lee Boulware, Megan Clarke, Mary-Carter Creech, Maryann Curran, Jill Dziko, Julie Fisher, Sandra Gormon-Brown, Gail Hardman-Woung, Lynne Hartman, Spring Hecht, Linnea Lauer, Gwen Lewis, Michele Schneidler, Linda Sheppard, Abbie Smith, Laura Stone, and Sandy Swan. Kudos to Brian Andersen, who makes organized consultation groups, continuing education credits, attachment certificate programs, and workshops happen. Friend and colleague, Susan Flick, read the early material, helping me with the tone. What a community!

I am a writer of other people's stories. This book shows the collected wisdom of my client families and their stories. While I have changed identifying information to protect confidentiality, I could not have written a solid book without their experiences.

My life has cohesion because of my faith. I am grateful to God for the fresh joy that I experience as I work with my gifts within the divine design. Less esoterically, it really must be due to the power of God that I somehow had the time to write this book!

My experience with Jessica Kingsley's editorial staff has been so positive! Thank you to Stephen Jones, Senior Editor, for your clarity in recognizing the joyful concepts in the material and for your guidance—from selection of the topic down to the voice of the book. Sarah Hull, and then Victoria Nicholas, kept the book's process organized and moving along—always interacting with grace. I will see you for lunch in London.

Notes to the reader

Facts in the anecdotes and vignettes have been altered to protect the confidentiality of clients.

The photos are of volunteers, not clients. They are much-appreciated friends with their families.

Introduction

This book is written simply and sprinkled with photos. It is meant to help you, as parents, to capture the warmth and fun of forming the closest of relationships—attachments—with your children. The book describes ways to love your child best—whether you are connecting to your child or setting limits. I want you and your child to grow together into your best selves.

I confess: I did not have a cohesive approach to my parenting when I first began. My information was piecemeal. Of course, I loved my children, but my older daughter once lamented: "I was the tester cookie. You thought, 'She's a little underdone here, burnt there, but we'll do better with the next ones.'" I hope that all you parents will benefit from my successes and my failures. By the time we master parenting, coming up with a solid, overall plan, it seems that our children are texting us instead of living with us! But in spite of my mistakes, I know that the close connections I enjoyed with my children certainly compensated for my weak areas. Some of the information in this book is grounded in the wonderful attachment and brain research that is now available, but was not there when I first parented. I am delighted to be able to include that material for parents.

This book looks at the heart of close connections. Using sensory-rich suggestions and photos, it will guide you through the "how-to" skill set of forming these connections (attaching). The book is valuable if you need your parenting course charted—or if you want reassurance that you are on the right track. If you are a parent who has never spent time with infants or small children, this book will give you skills to connect. If you have two children, one with an easy temperament and one with a challenging temperament, this book is for you. The book will help you use a compatible parenting approach for both children.

All of us, as parents, want to keep close connections when we have to limit or discipline our children. The book describes this skill. The book's suggestions are rooted in the latest brain research. The approaches will help your children, not only to connect with you, but to develop emotional intelligence and resilience throughout life.

If you have shared custody, or if you are a step-parent whose step-child is trying to connect to you, this book will provide a path for you. You may be an adoptive or foster parent, trying to understand how to parent a stressed child. This book will help you to nurture and limit, while remaining positive and kind. Maybe you are a person who had poor parenting in your growing-up years. The book's information will help you to develop healthy relationships with *your* children.

This book includes practical advice for children who are developing without any issues, as well as advice when the road is bumpier. It gives practical information on how to limit children, with an overall strategy on discipline. The book explains how to assist children who have problems with attention, memory, or impulsive behavior.

This book complements previous books, *Nurturing Adoptions: Creating Resilience after Neglect and Trauma* (Gray 2012a) and *Attaching in Adoption: Practical Tools for Today's Parents* (Gray 2012b). I would recommend these books as comprehensive guides to attachment, trauma, and therapy. This book is not adoption-specific, but it is adoption-friendly. It includes practical information on stress and higher-thinking skills in children, called executive functioning. It provides cutting-edge information in an easy-to-understand format.

Above all, this book gives to parents the skills and permission to enjoy the process of attaching and the pleasures of parenting—without the burden of having to be perfect.

Chapter 1

Close Connections

Bonding and Attachment

What did you picture when you thought of yourself parenting a child? Did you see yourself tenderly holding your baby or child, playing together, snuggling, holding hands, or reading books together at night? These are scenes of sharing the pleasure of being connected to your child—whether it is during a calming time as you snuggle up with a little one at bedtime or the exciting time of hide-and-seek.

Close connections, called attachments, are the day-to-day expressions of the mental pictures above. Our children cuddle. They save their special surprises for us, show delight at being with us, and feel safe and valued by us. You, their parents, are kind, strong, and sensitive. You set and enforce limits in a reasonable manner. Frustration is low—enjoyment high. Admittedly, parenting images like this are parenting at its best. Still, you should be able to anticipate a good portion of your time with your children to be just this way.

Gazing at each other, playing together, skin-to-skin contact, feeding times, and meeting needs in a sensitive way are ways to "bond." Over the course of months, as parents and children repeat these activities many times, they become exclusively bonded to each other. We refer to these exclusive and intimate bonds as "*attachments*." When your children believe that you will keep them safe, meet their needs, and that you are sensitive to their needs, the type of attachment that forms between you and your child is known as a "*secure*" attachment.

Attachments, by definition, are the closest of our relationships. They are *exclusive*. We are close with select people. People are not replaceable. We are attached to our family members, and our very best friends. We do not go up to just anybody for closeness, or to get our needs met. (If children do that, it is a danger sign.) Attachments are *emotional*. We feel strong emotions around the people to whom we are attached—love and joy when we are with them, fear and grief if our connection to them is threatened or if they are in danger. Attachments are *intimate*. Both physically and emotionally we open ourselves up to the other person in an attached relationship.

In our attached relationships with our children we provide for our children's needs. Usually people think of simple physical needs—food, warmth, and basic safety. Over the last four decades, research has described what my grandmothers knew well: through our attachments we teach our children the basics of understanding their emotional life and that of others. We provide a template for children to handle their own emotions through their emotional connection with us. In this next section we will discuss a bit of the "wiring" that occurs in your child's brain when you are connecting to your child.

How attachment shapes your child's brain

The relationship that you form with your child—it is hoped a secure attachment—influences your child's brain for the better. You are actually shaping your child's brain as you attach. As you are caring for your child, certain areas of your brain will be active. These are called "*neural firing patterns*." That is, "neural," referring to brain cells, and "firing," referring to the activity of these cells. The neurons, which have electrical signals, are "firing" in particular patterns.

Babies and children have brains that are shaped by their parents' brain patterns. When you are connecting with your baby or child, or if you are playing with or calming yourself or child, your brain will show activity in those brain areas that have to do with emotions and relationships. Amazingly, that will cause the corresponding areas of your baby or child's brain to become active. Your child's brain patterns are also called "neural firing patterns." The neural firing patterns of parents are mimicked or echoed by infants and small children. Over time, your baby or child will lay down wiring, causing their brain patterns to resemble yours. Through your relationship, you will shape their brains.

Ideally, your brain patterns of soothing, playfulness, or interest in your baby or child will be reflected by similar activity in the same regions of your child's brain. Since infant's and children's brains are just developing, these patterns become the early architecture of their brains. Your children literally become shaped by your brain patterns—whether or not there is a biological relationship. In secure attachments, children's brains reflect their parents' abilities of calming, compassion, and empathy, as well as stress reduction. They become "wired" to be social, caring, playful, and easier to calm. Over time these tend to become their personality traits. These are all brain-based developments in our children that naturally emerge just by our being caring, although imperfect, parents.

Secure attachments seem to emerge naturally when adults have had healthy models and when children have been treated well from birth. But secure attachments may need to be jump-started when you or your child are forming a relationship after a rocky start. Some of the basics to remember in forming a secure attachment with your child are being:

- kind

- capable (good basic physical care)

- sensitive

- stable

- imperfect—but willing to try again.

When we do the above, children feel:

- valued

- safe

- worth your attention and care

- deserving of love and care when they are challenging

- aware that when you have bad moments, you will try to remedy the moment and will rebound.

Children with secure attachments seem to have a sturdy quality to them. The children approach relationships with brain patterns of being confident and caring. They tend to be good at recognizing the emotions of others and of themselves. They tend to calm themselves more easily. They tend to be more confident in turning to others for help when needed. They are also more curious and ready to explore the world since they know that they have you to help them. They feel safe enough to venture out.

The term "security" in attachment also refers to the belief that people can count on each other to return after an absence. When you and your child need to be separated, you know that you will miss each other when you have to be apart. But, children learn that you return. And, that you will be sensitive to their needs—you will not be gone too long a time for them to tolerate at their age.

As your children get older, they learn that when you let each other down, you will model how to work on apologizing, and try to work out the problem. The connection between you will teach your children how to treat themselves and other people with respect and value. They will learn from you how to connect meaningfully to others—including the next generation.

(Take a moment to give yourself credit for caring about your relationship with your child, including taking the time to read this book.)

How long does it take to become attached?

If you are parenting and you do not feel the closeness that you had hoped for, you may start feeling worried or even distant. A woman confided: "I didn't fall in love with my baby. I thought that she was a little boring. I was embarrassed to tell anyone that I didn't feel the same love for my baby as my older daughter."

Some parents attach to their babies before birth or shortly after. On the infant's part, attachments develop over time—typically about six months for infants and toddlers, and six months to a year for preschoolers and older who enter into an attached relationship at that time. Some people feel an immediate rush of close feelings. Others go through the cycle of meeting their baby's needs over and over again, gradually feeling closer and closer. If you are one of the latter, you will find yourself continuing to give good care while the feelings are developing. The woman in the example above said:

> At about six months I realized that I had a loving, emotional connection to my baby. It took a while. Right after she was born, I thought that she might be placed with a different adoptive family, which probably stood in the way of my attaching right away. I was a little numb. I was content with the relationship with my older daughter, who was also adopted. It was hard to get used to having two children to juggle. Of course, I would never want it any other way, now. I love both my children. I felt too guilty to share with anyone that I was waiting to feel attached. It felt good to hear you say that it can take a while. It did in my family.

The intimacy of caring for a little one can gradually bring you and your child closer over time.

But using some of the techniques pictured and described in this chapter may help to increase your feelings of closeness, making connection easier.

Toddlers or children who join your family

If you are trying to attach to a child who was previously parented by someone else, it can be harder to feel connected, or even confident that you are meeting the little one's needs. As you try to meet their needs or understand what they want, you may find that they both reach towards you and push away. Or, they might seem to want something from you, but then fuss that it is the wrong thing. This is typical after children have been parented by insensitive or even frightening parents, or if they are grieving former parents. Babies or children may show their needs in a confusing manner. They may seem to reach towards you, and then draw away. Or, they may react in a confusing manner even when you do the right things. You can easily become discouraged. When it seems that your child does not like you or want the love that you are trying to give, try thinking that your child simply does not know how to form a close connection yet. It will take time and support for you to keep on trying.

It is hard not to take it personally when children or babies do not seem to like us. Sometimes they seem to be giving us the signal that we are doing the wrong things when we are trying to help them.

It can be reassuring to know that this is a common problem with babies and children who have been neglected or who are missing their former parents. Do your best to stay sensitive and caring for this little one who is so confused. But, at the same time, recognize that you are doing something that takes an emotional toll on you. It will help to give yourself support and breaks so that you stay caring and sensitive. It can take a while of giving, giving, and giving again until your child learns that you are caring and reliable.

If you have a solid parenting background, either by parenting other children or by being parented well, you may have to remind yourself that you have what it takes to attach to children. It simply may take doing the right thing for a longer period of time. If you are not sure that you are doing the right thing, it can help to consult with a professional. Everyone forming attachments after the newborn stage can use more emotional support. Most people, who only see a cute child or baby, will have no idea of how hard it can be to have the child push you away, or seem more upset than soothed when you try to care for them. If you want more information on this topic, *Attaching in Adoption: Practical Tools for Today's Parents* (Gray 2012b) is a book with specific information on attachment specific to children's ages and stages of development.

If you give yourself the advantage of time, forming a relationship with your child without the stress of needing to hurry, you will find it easier to think about your child sensitively and with joy. High stress makes it harder for any of us, as parents, to be sensitive to our children.

There is not a "critical window," or a "use it or lose it" window within which children *must* make attachments. If you were delayed in beginning the attachment process with your child, it means that you will have to be more intentional in forming attachments. Children are wired to want to connect to parents, and to want to respond to sensitive and responsive parenting. But after adverse situations in life, children may have difficulty responding in the way that parents expect. As mentioned earlier, they may have confusing or contradictory responses when parents reach out to caress, or look at children with a smile. This is typical for children who have had rough starts in life.[1] They want both to respond and to retreat. They are caught in the contradictions between their earlier and current parenting.

Children who have had fewer losses or stressful experiences usually have an easier time forming attachments. However, with some persistence and positivism, parents can woo even resistant little ones into secure attachments in the vast majority of cases.

Creating positive connections—emotional looping

Emotional looping happens when either you or your child does something to connect, the other responds, and the person who began the loop responds to the response. For example, the parent smiles, the child smiles back, and both smile, feeling good as they are aware of each other's feelings. Positive looping is an emotional skill that healthy families encourage. Some people seem to be enjoying their relationships almost all of the time. They both expect and receive a lot of positive looping from their children.

Children who have not experienced positive looping often have not yet learned to close an "emotional loop." The parent initiates their side of the loop and their child:

- ignores

- responds in a confusing way, with facial grimaces, or by batting at the parent

- responds *very* slowly like they are in slow motion

- moves away from their parent, or

- grabs their parent tightly—as if capturing them.

In healthy relationships, you can expect to close many, many positive loops with your child every day. A typical day might be 15 hugs, 100 "eyes and smiles" loops (as described in the paragraph above), 50 positive touches or gestures, and so forth. But for children unused to the language of love, the loops are often unclosed. Children might have learned to "show off" in a cute way,

---

1   Bernard, K. and Dozier, M. (2011) "This Is My Baby: Foster Parents' Feelings of Commitment and Displays of Delight." *Infant Mental Health Journal,* 32(2): 252–262.

but do not know how to respond when parents begin the loop. You may send a message of love in the form of a loving touch or nice comment, but your child may look dazed, ignore you, act kind of goofy, or look away.

The unclosed loops can cause you, the parent, to feel rather flat. You may have to fortify your own self-esteem, realizing that children are simply responding with what they have learned, or not learned, previously. It will take you, as the parent, some time to change your child's reality—that you want to connect with them and that you are emotionally accessible. Tasha is an example of the development of emotional looping. Her mother said:

> She was sick when she came to us at a year old. She had early developmental tests. The results were *very* discouraging; she was as responsive as a spud. We were scared, but stubborn. When she was feeling better, we spent a lot of time on the floor, with eye contact, playing with her, and getting her attention again when she'd look away. Within six months she was responsive, laughing a lot, and playful. When she'd been with us a year, we shredded her first developmental tests over a glass of champagne. She's a confident third grader now—and a snuggle bug.

Most parents feel rather let-down and rejected when their children do not respond in a loving manner. If you are not getting the response that you want, then of course you will feel sad. It is normal to want a loving relationship with your little one. But it is typical for parents to muster warmth, enduring children's negative reactions after these same children have been through a series of foster homes, poor treatment, or through custody struggles.

Even if you are the most chipper parent, you will feel like drawing back when you get a confusing or mixed response. But if you can stay the course, the research shows that you are likely to have the relationship that you long for in the majority of cases.[2,3] It will take persistence and patience to keep doing loving, sensitive, parenting. It is normal to want positive looping. But, you may have

2   Fisher, P. and Kim, H. (2007) "Intervention Effects on Foster Preschoolers' Attachment-Related Behaviors from a Randomized Trial." *Prevention Science,* 8(2): 161–170.

3   Bates, B. and Dozier, M. (2002) "The Importance of Maternal State of Mind Regarding Attachment and Infant Age at Placement to Foster Mothers' Representations of Their Foster Infants." *Infant Mental Health Journal,* 23(4): 417–431.

to wait until your child learns how to respond to a loving parent. And, you may have to increase the positive intensity of your end of the looping.

But how do you know if you are missing something, doing something wrong, or, whether you simply need to try longer at being a loving, sensitive parent? The next section describes techniques that encourage attachment. You are invited to see how many of the techniques you use now, which ones you would like to add, or whether you are doing enough.

Techniques that encourage attachment

Eye contact with your child encourages attachment. After making eye contact, you can follow up with a smile. Think warm thoughts that cause warm feelings towards your child when you make eye contact. Children's brains can tell the difference between "real" emotional availability and the polite, distracted signals of a preoccupied parent. Since attachment is a brain-to-brain connection, the appropriate brain areas of parents' brains need to be activated in order for children to feel the connection. What we have found is that we must engage the emotional parts of *our* brains in order to engage the emotional parts of *their* brains. If we are going through the motions, but with our minds elsewhere, we will not connect. Relaxing and enjoying the moment will engage the "right" parts of our minds.

What does it look like when you are connecting through eye contact? Figures 1.1(a), 1.1(b), 1.2(a), 1.2(b), 1.3(a), and 1.3(b) show eye contact with real emotional connection.

Figure 1.1(a): Inviting eye contact.

Figure 1.1(b): Inviting eye contact.

Figure 1.2(a): Eyes and smile.

Figure 1.2(b): Eyes and smile.

Figure 1.3(a): Eye contact in Figure 1.1(a) results in a hug and smile.

Figure 1.3(b): Eyes, smile, and hug.

In the photos there are pictures of a parent who is giving a signal, to have eye contact and smiles from their child. The sig. is simply a tilt of the head followed by the smile. Notice that the parent in the first photo is smiling.

When asking for eye contact from children, it works best if your "ask" is accompanied by a smile. If children do not respond, try to make the smile a game. Move your head into funny positions to get eye contact. Perhaps you will try getting on the floor, looking up. Stay playful, not morose or dejected. For the older child, for example, you might use words like "You are letting my smile fall on the floor. Let's pick it up and put it in your love tank." Tap your chest to indicate the "love tank" or heart. Parents can elaborate on this theme. "How many hearts do you think are in there? Do you have just one smile in your love tank? Do you have a hug to put in your love tank?" Tapping our heart area, our chest area, seems to wake up the feelings in us and in our children.

When children are just learning to form eye contact, I like to have a signal that indicates "Look at me." I tap the bridge of my nose with a smile. The ability to maintain eye contact is neurologically based. That means that our brains need to develop the capacity to gaze at another person. Often children are simply unable to look at parents for very long without feeling overwhelmed. It is typical for children to look, look away, look, and once again look away. As adults, we can relate to needing breaks from gaze. When we are feeling shy or overwhelmed, we will look away. Most of us look away less now that we have developed the necessary brain wiring to hold our gaze.

Encourage a playful, positive, learning curve during which your child gradually develops the ability to gaze (look) at you, with a smile and response. Figure 1.4 shows a person asking for a responsive smile from a child, while tapping their nose as a signal to ask for the smile with eye contact. Notice that the request is one that is done playfully.

Figure 1.4: Eyes, tapping of nose, and smile.

Cuddling, snuggling, and feeling cozy

Can you remember being snuggled up to a parent or grandparent? How safe and valued you felt!

Parents yearn to give children these cozy experiences. But when infants or children are coming to parents after being in other homes, those children may still be grieving. The grief will cause them to withdraw or push away. Shock will cause them to look "dazed" and to act unresponsively. Parents may have the experience of snuggling a child who simply does not respond for quite a while.

Or, perhaps you are a parent who was depressed for a time. When you are doing better, you realize that you have a child who is not responsive. They may look a bit depressed as well. That, in itself, can feel really depressing! Parents have every right to feel a bit let down if their children do not respond. Having a little compassion for yourself is just fine. But take a step back, having compassion for both yourself and your child, recognizing that it is not your or your child's fault that they are non-responsive. It might take teaching them how to nestle, or supporting them through grief, before they can cuddle, enjoy sitting with you, or feel fully present instead of looking dazed or withdrawing. It is important for parents not to stay angry at either themselves or their children. We may end up expressing the anger by pulling away. That is not being true to ourselves or our children.

Some children have never learned to snuggle. Instead, they do not cling or hold on in a comfortable manner. Even when they are trying to hug or lap-sit as other children do, somehow they do not mold to their parents. If this is your child, let them know by words or body language that they are welcome in your lap. But you should also feel free to rearrange them in a manner that is comfortable for you. Over time they will learn to sit comfortably as they develop some muscle memory for sitting with you (see Figures 1.5(a) and 1.5(b)).

Even if parents have the desire to show physical affection towards their children, some children have a reaction to touch because of *sensory sensitivities*. People with sensory sensitivities find the typical range of stimulation is overwhelming for them, or too little stimulation for them. They feel anxious and injured when overstimulated, or press into parents when seeking stimulation.

These children may hang onto parents, swinging on them as if the parents are pieces of furniture. While most children do this from time to time, these kids are non-stop. Others may say, "Ouch, that hurts!" when parents have hugged them with normal pressure. A particular child's sensitivities may change throughout the day. If yours if such a child, please try not to take these reactions personally. You can take a minute, finding the comfortable spacing between you and your child. I suggest being sensitive to your child's needs, without being apologetic when you are outside their comfort zone. The attitude is a patient, "Help me to help us get this right."

Children with attention deficit disorder with hyperactivity (ADHD) may snuggle, wiggle, and run off. I like to encourage them to come back for a little more time. Sometimes they have simply forgotten what they were doing. It is not a personal rejection. Later, a child with ADHD may say, "I never get to cuddle with you, Daddy." If invited to come back, they can return and look at the book together with you or hear the rest of the song you were singing with them. Children with attention issues will often have more movements, even if listening or snuggling. I suggest that you attempt to overlook the wiggling. If sitting quietly and calmly is a requirement for snuggles with you, your child with attention deficit disorder may be quite limited in how long they are able to be with you. Instead, enjoy the child you have—wiggles, giggles, and all (see Figures 1.6(a) and 1.6(b)).

Figure 1.5(a): Child cuddling with parent.

Figure 1.5(b): Child cuddling with parent.

Figure 1.6(a): Child cuddling and wiggling with parent.

Figure 1.6(b): Child cuddling and wiggling with parent.

Stroking hands and rubbing feet

The inside of our palms and the arches of our feet are areas of the body that alert people to attachment "cues." These attachment "cues" are "signals" that cause people to respond with interest in a close relationship. When you are talking to children, and if you want to increase the positive signals for attachment, you can stroke the inside of your child's palm (see Figures 1.7(a) and 1.7(b)). It will signal your child to look towards your eyes. The touch is a comforting, pleasant stroke on a child's or baby's palms. Sometimes children pull their hands away. If that happens to you, you can turn the touch into a game. Hold out your hands, allowing your child to place their hands on top. Then put one of your hands on top of their hand. They can put their free hand on top of yours. The game goes faster and faster, with you and your child racing to get your hand on top. The game finishes with laughing. Often children will say, "Let's do it again!" This little game still allows for palm contact without children feeling that they are being "grabbed."

When reading or talking to children, parents may want to rub their children's feet (see Figures 1.8(a) and 1.8(b)). The foot-stroking is soothing. Again, it helps connect children to parents. Some parents rub lotions or shea butter into their children's skin, rubbing the soles of their feet in the process.

Figure 1.7(a): Palm-stroking when talking to child.

Figure 1.7(b): Palm-stroking when talking to child.

Figure 1.8(a): Foot-stroking when talking to child.

Figure 1.8(b): Foot-stroking resulting in eye contact and closeness.

Cheek-stroking and temple-stroking

One of the most intimate parental touches is light touching of our children's faces. You can use a soothing touch by lightly stroking the side of your baby or child's face, from the top of the head along the outside of the temples. You can use this type of touch when calming a little one who is overstimulated or resisting sleep.

Similarly, a light stroking of your baby or child's cheeks is a cue for attachment (see Figures 1.9(a) and 1.9(b)). You are invited to try this touch in front of a mirror. Try stroking a few times in a sweeping, upward motion half-way between the corner of your mouth and ear. The motion is centered on where dimples are on cheeks—whether or not you have dimples. This stroking causes babies to search for the nipple—either of the bottle or breast, depending on how they are being fed.

Since feeding and attachment are so strongly linked, stroking cheeks will signal children to respond by connecting to parents. Throughout the life cycle, cheek-stroking remains an intimate behavior that promotes attachment. Children typically look for their parent's eyes when their cheeks are being stroked. It is wired into our most basic systems. Touching cheeks is so intimate that few people are permitted this type of intimate touch. It tends to be reserved for parents and children, grandparents and grandchildren, siblings, or intimate couples.

In the first months of life, babies will automatically turn to the side of the cheek-stroking to suck or to eat. If you are parenting a baby who is under eating, or dozing through feedings because of prematurity or drug exposure, you can use this stroking to encourage your baby to wake up to finish eating. It is similarly effective in waking up babies or children to your interest in a close relationship with them.

Figure 1.9(a): Cheek-stroking.

Figure 1.9(b): Cheek-stroking.

Mealtimes and feeding

Eating together is a wonderful way to promote attachment. For attachment purposes, and just the joy of life, meals should be enjoyable times during which everyone relaxes around the food. I suggest that it is a "neutral zone" in which inflammatory topics are avoided. Discussions over whether or not the children fought, the amount of homework they have, or whether chores are done or not, should be deferred. The meal is not a business meeting for the family, but a time of emotional connection.

Ideally, parents should sit down with children at the table, relaxing as they take their seats. It is best if at least two out of the three meals are unhurried. Urging children to "hurry," "finish," or eat more or less of a dish are prompts best avoided. Instead, mention how positive the flavors are—with shared enjoyment and eye contact. Or, mention how pleasant it is to eat with your family. For negative reactions to dishes, parents may say, "Not your favorite." Or, "Your taste buds have not developed for that taste—maybe next year."

The point is to establish the link between food, attachment, and pleasure. Fear or anxiety will influence appetite negatively. The pleasure and relationship emphasis on sharing food will also help reluctant eaters or children with sensory sensitivities. The latter often find chewing, strong flavors, textures, and swallowing to be difficult. A relaxed atmosphere helps them to overcome some of their struggles around food.

Some children approach meals with issues. Perhaps your child has complications due to sensory issues (the food feels like the wrong texture or the taste is too intense), or food scarcity (a background of too little food and at unpredictable times), or a difference in body rhythms due to stress (not hungry in the morning or ravenous at non-meal times). These things can be extremely stressful to any parent. You may find yourself migrating from a steady, pleasant way of providing meals to becoming anxious and controlling as you anticipate your child's lack of appetite or finicky reaction to the food you have prepared.

Children who have a background of food scarcity will have many issues around food and attachment. If you are parenting such a child, it will help your child if you make a point of preparing and providing meals in a reliable and obvious manner. They will notice that you take seriously your responsibility of providing food. Feeding every two to three hours for smaller children or every three to four hours for older children will enable your children to recognize you as a trustworthy attachment figure. As long as children have to remind parents about meals, children still maintain the responsibility of feeding themselves. Parents who are sensitive to this potent issue will plan for meals in an obvious manner. (There is a more complete discussion of feeding and mealtimes in upcoming chapters.)

Skin-to-skin contact, breast- or bottle-feeding and attachment

Babies enjoy having skin-to-skin contact while they feed. Breast-feeding provides this skin-to-skin contact as well as producing oxytocin in the mother, which stimulates attachment. Oxytocin is a hormone that is released during breast-feeding, skin-to-skin contact, lovemaking, and cuddling. It is sometimes called the "love hormone." There is some theoretical information that oxytocin production may help mothers to reduce some of the frustration/anger from the stressors that are part of parenting.[4] Skin-to-skin contact, as Figures 1.10(a) and 1.10(b) illustrate, assists bonding between parents and children.

---

4   Fonagy, P., Luyten, P., and Strathearn, L. (2011) "Borderline Personality Disorder, Mentalization, and the Neurobiology of Attachment." *Infant Mental Health Journal,* 32(1): 47–69.

Figure 1.10(a): Skin-to-skin.

Figure 1.10(b): Skin-to-skin.

For many of you who are forming attachments, particularly fathers, breast-feeding is not going to happen. Figures 1.11 (a–c) show bottle-feeding for attachment purposes. But even if children are beyond the bottle stage, skin-to-skin contact and bottle-feeding for attachment purposes may be helpful if your child has come to you later in childhood and is struggling to have a connection with you. Children up to the age of eight may still benefit from this technique if they had significant neglect (Figure 1.11(d)). Of course, this would not be forced on a child, but could be offered as a once- or twice-daily close time with a parent. Over a few months children may transition to reading times, play, or other high-connection activities.

Figure 1.11(a): Bottle-feeding for attachment purposes

Figure 1.11(b): Bottle-feeding for attachment purposes

Figure 1.11(c): Bottle-feeding for attachment purposes

Figure 1.11(d): Bottle-feeding older child for attachment purposes.

The parents of smaller children may want to introduce a cozy lap time, with fathers taking their shirts off during bottle-feeding time. Use apple juice in a bottle with a small hole in the nipple. Allow the child to enjoy the emotional and sensory sensations of sweet juice, sucking, skin contact, and your soothing presence. Many parents rock during this time, if their child likes rocking. For attachment purposes, parents can rock and bottle-feed once or twice a day for 15 minutes, even if their child is beyond the normal bottle stage.

Children sometimes take the bottle, hop off the parent's lap, and walk around with the bottle hanging out of their mouths. This rather defeats the purpose. If you are using bottle-feeding to encourage attachment, then it is just fine to be the one who holds the bottle. Sing to your little one, smiling with eye contact, during the lap time. Often your child may wiggle and move to get off your lap in less time than 15 minutes. Following your little one's lead into a play time is a great transition. The idea is to build positive looping and connections, so you are still winners as you connect in different ways.

Play's fusing power

Play is one of the most enjoyable ways to build attachment with children or babies. Our brains are particularly wired to respond to play that includes:

- high excitement

- movement

- exaggerated expressions

- creativity

- body contact or close, shared physical space.

Sometimes children have not yet learned how to play. If you are parenting such a child, it can be startling to realize that your child does not seem to know how to have fun with you. Most of us think that childhood and playfulness naturally go together. Trying to play with children who are just learning to play may feel flat and one-sided for a while.

Over time, your child will come to seek out your company and understand the back-and-forth, or mutuality of play. At first, they might be at a developmental stage where they want to play beside you but not with you. It is typical that they want to be controlling in their play. (Controlling others is a step in development before controlling ourselves.) Add some zest and excitement in the play as your child gets used to playing with you. Add elaboration and imagination, without completely taking over the play.

There are lots of games that build attachment and relationships. Play that includes drama and physical closeness will be particularly good at building relationships. Any variation of hide-and-seek tends to be fun. This can be as simple as hiding behind the edge of a baby blanket for a baby or later hiding and counting for a preschooler. Games of hide-and-seek are classic attachment games. All of us want to be worth the chase! Use zest and mock surprise to build excitement during the chase. Other favorite play options are:

- "Airplane" rides in which the parent is the airplane and the child takes a ride (see Figure 1.12).

- Water games that involve jumping off the parent's shoulders, jumping into the parent's arms, or fun with pool "noodles."

- "Piggyback rides," which may evolve over time to "trips" to other parts of the house and then imaginary kingdoms.

- Tickle games that include a sense of anticipation and giggly excitement by children. (Do not tickle to the extent that children feel helpless.)

Figure 1.12: "Airplane" ride.

The games build excitement and allow you to share excitement and pleasure. The excitement, or "high arousal" followed by pleasurable experiences, is a cycle that builds attachment.

There are little hairs in the inner ear (hair cell stereocilia) that respond when children are tipped or moved, as they are during activities like "airplane rides," when parents swing children, or when they jump off dad's shoulders in the pool. The movement of these little hairs is believed to be a signal for attachment.[5] They are another way in which we are "hard-wired" for attachment.

Some parents are so intentional about attachment that they tend to do the games in a serious manner. They act as if playing with their children is one more item on their "to-do" list. The zip is gone. This rather spoils the experience. I suggest that parents enjoy the moment, giving themselves up to the spirit of the play, re-capturing some their own favorite childhood moments. If you are having trouble getting a sense of joy as you play with your child, remember your own favorite childhood memories. It helps to borrow these memories to seed your play with a joyful attitude, even if it takes your child some time to catch up with your enthusiasm.

Physical play tends to be an open door for children and parents who are forming attachments. If you are a tired or worried parent, you may notice a tendency to select structured play, like puzzles. Puzzles are wonderful as a calming activity. But to stimulate children who are harder to connect with, physical play is a more successful activity. It allows the high excitement that fuses the connection between the two of you.

Children who have been moved between families, or who have weathered stressful beginnings, tend to run high cortisol levels, which is a measure of the stress that they are feeling. These cortisol levels ready their bodies for a physical reaction—fight or flight. This physical play gives children an outlet for the energy that their bodies are producing. Play simultaneously helps them to feel better and helps them to attach. Parents who try physical play, and who let themselves get caught up in the spirit of it, find their stress reduced as they enjoy physical play. I used to run around the outside of a king-sized bed, trying to grab my children's ankles or tickle their

---

5   Foster, C. (1988) All-day Training on Attachment, Seattle, WA.

feet as they bounced on the bed. Even though I might have been preoccupied with other thoughts at the beginning of the game, I soon was laughing and relaxed with the children as they dove and jumped away. Without much effort I could morph into a lion, dog, or other creature in order to spice up the play. I benefitted more than the children!

Play builds brains

It is also worth noting the value of play in other developmental areas that ultimately help children in their social relationships and overall functioning. Researchers have found that play is a useful way to build skills such as sustaining attention, planning, and self-monitoring that are called "executive functioning." There is a detailed description of executive functioning in Chapter 4, but a few aspects will be described here. Play helps the following aspects of executive functioning: staying with a theme, understanding the point of view of another and adapting to that point of view, flexibility, and inhibiting impulses.

Play can help children to learn to preplan as they make a plan for their play. (For example: "Let's play elves. We will get Mom's old jewelry for treasure. I will be the queen and you will be the court elf.") They learn better attention by staying with a play topic. Children must keep their play partners satisfied, which helps with flexibility and understanding the other's point of view. They must control their impulses by practicing inhibiting impulses in order to stay with the play themes.

Rather than supplying children with many props, watching them play, it is better for the developing mind to have fewer props, so that children have to imagine and remember the themes within the play. This approach helps with the development of working memory, as in the example of Sophia, below.

> In my office Sophia, aged eight years old, wanted to play out a shopping trip with her mother. (In real life, her shopping trips with either parent often included control battles.) Sophia wanted to pretend that she was a teen, with a teen's interests in clothes. As Sophia first began to play, she was anxious about losing the thread of meaning of the play. She insisted that she needed many props—from wigs and lipstick to proper

purses. Sophia's concerns were valid. She had a hard time remembering themes, staying on track, or imagining. Sophia and her mother decided to write out her play plan. Her mother and I *noticed* when Sophia checked to make certain that her mother was in agreement with the way the play would unfold. This helped Sophia to repeat these successful collaborative, polite check-ins. Sophia was able to compose a play that stressed listening to each other and compromise.

Over time, Sophia used the play as a means to introduce losses and relationships struggles. She increasingly used her imagination to make props out of items that were present in the room. Over a six-month period she improved in inhibiting distracting themes. "That's off-topic," she would announce. She used her mother as a model in learning to satisfy her play partner's wishes when playing together. She asked me to play parts by checking them out with me, saying, "Deborah, would you mind?" Sophia also used a plan to guide the overall play. These developments showed in other areas of her life—academic and social.

While the example above was one from my therapy practice, parents can easily use these suggestions at home. Play can help your children in remembering themes, using their imaginations, and adapting the play to keep everyone having a good time. Play also helps children to feel closer and more attuned (on the same emotional wavelength) to their parents.

Bedtime and morning routines

Children need a little more support at bedtime. Almost all children are afraid to be alone in the dark. Providing a bit more security helps them douse that fear. A good routine strengthens attachment security in children. Your presence provides the basis for relaxing and feeling secure. Most parents and children do best with a set, nighttime ritual.

Many of you had nice rituals with your parents, so have a mental pattern of what that looks and feels like. The notion of a night or early morning snuggle time sounds self-evident. You experienced these happy, "tuck-in" rituals. Some of you missed these pleasant bedtimes. You have no idea what it really looks like. Typically, the rituals in the evening consist of approximately 15 minutes in a rocking chair, or with your child in your lap, or sitting close beside you. You may be sitting on your child's bed. You read, sing, or tell stories to your child and tell them that they are loved. The tone of the parent is a relaxed one, with a rhythmic voice. (Resist the urge to wrestle or toss your children around. That is for earlier in the day.) Since the supposition is that your children will already be tired at bedtime, they will become even more compliant with the notion of bedtime as they calm beside you and get sleepy. Soothe children towards sleep.

Parents who are building children's spiritual development may say night prayers with their children. (Do *not* say the morbid prayer, "If I should die before I wake, I pray the Lord my soul to take." Who sleeps after that?) These prayers should be upbeat. They ask for divine help with problems. Children ask for and accept forgiveness for nasty actions of the day. You assist children in asking for blessings, help, and forgiveness. Your night prayers build a sense of security in children and compassion for others.

After night stories and prayers, your little one is tucked into bed. You can fold the bedclothes under your child's feet, making a warm little pouch for the feet during cool weather. You kiss and hug your child in bed, and then leave with the lights on or off, depending on your child.

When children make "curtain calls," it is to be expected. If your child settles right into bed, you are lucky. If children reappear, keep returning them to bed without additional stories, songs, or drama. There is evidence that noisy environments really do keep children awake, so try to diminish background noise. In noisy homes children can lack sleep to the extent that academic work and attention suffer.[6] Some parents use the family bed model, with co-sleeping. But that still involves different bedtimes for parents and children, and the inevitable protest at the difference between bedtimes.

You may stroke your child's face lightly, along the temple and across the cheekbones, as a way for them to close their eyes and fall asleep. Using soothing smells can also help to calm children. Parents may want to slip their own pillowcase, which still has the parent's

---

6   Tininenko, J., Fisher, P., Bruce, J., and Pears, K. (2010) "Sleep Disruption in Young Foster Children." *Child Psychiatry and Human Development*, 41(4): 409–424.

scent on it, onto their child's pillows. Your smell helps to soothe your child. You can also give your child your t-shirt (worn to the point that it smells like you) to sleep with or wear. Many children do much better falling asleep with their parent's t-shirt over them. They feel more secure with the smell of their parent close by.

It can be challenging to muster the energy to finish the day well with your children. While you may be wishing for a few minutes to yourself, you can still enjoy the bedtime routine with your child. If you find yourself exhausted and barking at your child at bedtime, try to defer or give up some tasks so that you are able to enjoy the evening routine with your little one. These are important times for attachment. In our household, we typically ignored phone calls during our children's evening routine. We avoided more than one night a week of community or work activity that would take a parent away during bedtime hours. Frankly, this seemed largely to be about our self-preservation. As children get overtired, they can become even harder to settle.

Morning rituals can be as important as the nighttime cuddle story time. Especially for children who are anxious or controlling, the morning ritual helps them to "borrow" some of your emotional balance. Some rocking time in the morning, as you talk with your child about the day, will help these little ones to relax their need to control. In the morning cuddle you can "fill up" your child emotionally for the day. You can also help them to organize the day mentally. It helps children to feel confident and prepared. If there is a little problem or worry, it is easy to problem-solve during that morning time.

High stress and sleep

Children should be able to wake up without an alarm if they are getting enough sleep. After having had losses or trauma, children typically have a biorhythm that makes them want to stay up at night and sleep late into the mornings.[7] (This is normal for teens, not a sign of trauma by itself.) Parents can be patient with themselves and

---

7   Fisher, P., Gunnar, M., Dozier, M., Bruce, J., and Pears, K. (2006) "Effect of Therapeutic Interventions for Foster Children on Behavioral Problems, Caregiver Attachment, and Stress Regulatory Neural Systems." *Annals New York Academy of Sciences* d.o.i. 10.1196: 1–11.

their children if this is the case. It is not their fault or their child's. However, everyone does need to get into the process of reversing this pattern.

I have parents sit outside their children's room, with a book or a laptop as company, in preparation for a prompt return of their children to their rooms. In that way, the excursions through the house are more limited. It usually only takes a couple of weeks before children remain in their rooms. After an illness, these children may revert to the same nocturnal exploring. Parents can simply repeat the process of waiting outside the door, and as children emerge, they are returned to bed promptly. Scared children recognize that parents are "on guard," which reassures them. But they get no reward for coming out. They will simply be returned with low drama. With older children, I often give a reward if they do not try to come out of their rooms. Those rewards can be a piece of gum or a sticker at the kitchen table in the morning.

When children do not want to go to sleep, parents can become a little desperate during the nighttime ritual. They resort to subterfuge. As children begin to nod off, even typically dignified adults will actually crawl out of their children's rooms on all fours. I do not recommend sneaking out of your children's rooms as they are falling asleep. Over time, it simply makes them more reluctant to doze off. Children believe that they need to stay alert.

Parents who sneak away confirm children's beliefs that parents cannot be trusted and should be controlled. Instead, set the timer for the length of time that you will be staying in the bedroom. (Use a timer with a pleasant rather than a jarring end note.) The time on the timer will be spent on a night ritual and saying "good night." When the time is over, you, the parents, exit. Again, you may have to remain right outside the door until children accept the inevitable. I suggest using a kind, but firm manner. Sometimes we get tired and anxious ourselves, and begin to over talk, and then beg our children to "please, please go to sleep." This is overwhelming or upsetting to an already tired and cranky child. When our actions are clear and decisive, they speak better than words.

Anxious children do much better when they have steady routines with predictable schedules and ample nurturing from parents. Using affection, kind voices, timers, posted schedules (pictures or words) and routines will help them to reverse a cortisol pattern that keeps them up at night and sleepy in the morning. Getting into a negatively dramatic pattern of threatening, pleading, spanking, and so on will only keep night cortisol levels high, making the pattern harder to break.

Even though it is hard, parents should remain matter-of-fact with roaming children. Dramas delay the calming pattern that parents are trying to establish at bedtime. Also, the point of the nighttime routine is to promote security and connection in children. Yelling at children or pleading with children ("Please, please, we are going to be exhausted in the morning, I can't take this anymore...") will not give your children a sense of nighttime calm. And, children who are more on the controlling side tend to think that their persistent efforts are finally paying off. Success is near. Parents are flagging. Bedtime is negotiable!

Sleep is critical to healthy development. It helps with attention, behavior, and memory consolidation. (Memory consolidation means that newly learned information is woven into longer-term memory so that it can be accessed when needed.) Telling children who are a bit older the "why" of sleep helps them to realize that they are being cared for, not consigned to bed and boredom. This does not mean that they will comply, but the heart will go out of their protest.

Many adopted children have worries about birth relatives or others. These worries come out at night. Part of night reassurance is hearing about these worries and making a plan. If parents do night prayers, they can ask for help for these people. For example, one six-year-old girl prayed regularly for street children, since she used to be one. As an 11-year-old she and her family helped to collect and fill donated backpacks for children on the streets. She felt that she was part of a larger endeavor, and that she did not have to worry alone about the street friends she had left behind. Sensitivity to these issues will build attachment.

Enjoying the moment, "being present" when with our children

Our children need us, as parents, to show that we are holding them in our hearts and minds. They need the stability that our presence gives to them. We want them to know that we are available emotionally and available to interpret their world. When with our children, we should be mentally present, that is "in the moment," and aware of our children's emotions and interests about 30 per cent of the time.[8] While that seems like a low number, more focus than that tends to be a little dangerous in terms of driving, cooking, catching the bus, shopping, and so forth. Less time than that tends to be not enough for our children to feel that they are worth our attention.

Distraction is a problem in our society right now. Our smart phones and tablets make our daily lives quite interesting. But, our children cannot compete successfully for our attention. More and more, parents can be seen being with their children, but not truly present with their children. The children look blank and bored; the parents are preoccupied. Multitasking is not productive when forming and maintaining secure attachments. As parents we will need to silence the phone or tablet so that we are not distracted by every text, call, or message. Our children simply cannot move at the speed of the signals coming from our electronics. They will need to act out or give up in the face of it.

While watching some children in Washington Square in New York City, I noticed how often the children would walk behind their nannies for almost all of their time at the park, not complaining, as the nannies spoke on their phones. I mentioned this to my daughter. She said, "They don't protest—it's normal for them not to get attention." When parents are constantly on their cell phones or tablets, children often look blank or irritated. They show neither joy nor the positive emotional attunement of children whose parents are relating to them. While it is uncomfortable to see children fuss and protest, it is better than the quiet acceptance when they know that it does no good to protest.

---

8   Fosha, D. (2004) "Attachment Through the Lens of Affect: Implications for Clinical Practice, Accelerated Experiential–Dynamic Psychotherapy." Presentation in Seattle, WA.

The time with your child is supposed to be rich in helping with the development of their positive moods. Babies and children should be learning emotional tools for connecting with you and others. Pretending to be mentally present, but actually being emotionally somewhere else, will not result in activating the relationship areas of their brain. Instead, your child will not feel connected with you. You are critical to your child's development. I suggest that you value yourself and your child to the extent that you protect the importance of your time together.

Language skills are strengthened in attached relationships

Language development in your children typically tracks the enrichment of your homes—the conversational quality between you and your children. In an enriched environment children are learning:

- words to connect emotionally with others

- words to express their feelings and those of others

- language that describes their thoughts and those of others, and how those thoughts connect to feelings

- listening skills that will develop into adapted responses based on other people's interests or feelings.

All of these skills require the "laboratory" of parents or other attuned adults who are included by the parents in their children's lives.

The abilities listed above help children in problem-solving and calming. Just by naming feelings, children and adults will calm and begin to use better coping strategies. The listening skills assist children to become adults who are able to care for the emotional well-being of those close to them.

Listening and responding in an emotionally in-tune manner are abilities that you can help create in your child. In your relationships, you will usually be sensitive, patient, and in-tune with your child. That will help your child learn to respond in the same way. As your child's is able to listen, respond, and adapt conversations in an interesting manner, a positive feedback loop develops. Their emotional and language abilities promote friendships and secure attachments throughout life.

In secure attachments, people learn to speak in a way that allows others to feel emotionally safe and respected. Children who learn to put their feelings into language, and to respond with care and interest to others' feelings/interests, go on to build better relationships. These relationships skills show up as early as preschool. They continue as children, teens, and then adults use their skills in the world at large—creating healthy communities.

When children learn to listen and respond to people, recognizing others' interests and feelings, while still maintaining their own interests and feelings, they have achieved a milestone in emotional intelligence. At around six years of age we like to see children hold their point of view and that of another at the same time. From there they can move on to adapt to meet the needs of both parties. For example, let's take rock, paper, and scissors. The winner will chose the first game, but the other person chooses the second game. Quality relationships require that the interests of both parties are satisfied. This is an intricate skill-set that requires the development of a language of emotions and relationships. The early language skills that you build with your children will help them to stay with a topic, to compromise, and to express disappointments without howling or stomping off.

If you engage in conversations with your children, helping them to discuss their feelings or interests, as well as listen to others' feelings and interests, you equip your children to connect deeply both within the family, and with friends and future family members.

A sample conversation, developing these language skills, sounds like this in five-year-old John.

> "I want to play with all of my dinosaurs when Julian comes over. But he always wants to play superhero. I keep telling Julian that I don't like when he's the Hulk, but he does it anyway."
>
> Dad says, "It sounds like you are both frustrated."
>
> "I am," says John. "When he visited last time I told him that it was time to go home if he just wanted to be Hulk."
>
> Then Mom says, "That's not polite. Why don't you find something that you both enjoy?" John continues, "I don't understand why he doesn't even try dinosaurs."

"What do you do when he is Hulk?" Dad asks.

"I'm supposed to be the bad guy and run away," John says. "I don't want to be the guy who runs away. I don't like to be the bad guy when he's the Hulk. He gets to be the good guy."

Dad says, "Maybe you could tell Julian that it makes you feel frustrated that he's a good guy and he's the one with the superpowers."

John says, "I need to tell him that. It's not fun to have to run around and act afraid. I never get to be a superhero. We need to pick a game where we both get a chance to be a good guy. I could play another game even if he doesn't like dinosaurs. I just don't want to be a bad guy all of the time. I'll tell Julian."

"That sounds like a good idea," Dad says.

This is the type of conversational coaching that allows children to develop emotional language that is respectful. It opens space for compromise. The dad in the example above helped his son to identify his feelings and the reason behind his feelings. Notice that the parent did not try to solve the problem by dropping the friend. Instead he helped his son to develop skills to stay connected to another child.

By practicing language skills, children are able to find and use those words in real-life situations. A ten-year-old talked with his mother and me about the way in which his mother's tone scared him.

"She uses a mean voice with a big sigh. I feel like she hates me—like I did the most awful thing in the world when I just forgot to wipe off the counter after my snack. She sounds like Darth Vader."

"I'm sorry that I did that," his mother said. "I was raised in a loud and rough home. Sometimes my parents' voices pop out."

We agreed that the next time that she used "the voice" he would say: "Would you please use your regular voice? You're scaring me."

A few days later "the voice" emerged. He tentatively asked her to stop scaring him. His mother immediately stopped, exhaled, and asked kindly instead.

This simple intervention helped with the security of their attachment. It did not take a clinical wizard to accomplish the change—only a willing parent. Often you can ask a friend or family member for honest feedback about whether your tone of voice is scary, or whether your "busyness" makes you behave irritably with your children. People do not have to enter a therapy office to get common-sense advice.

When forming secure attachments, you may find that it takes some daring to trust in the power of kindness and compassion. Sometimes we have the sneaking thought that being a little mean or frightening might cause children to "snap to it" with less effort on our part. But secure attachment does not mean that you, as the parents, are weak, or cannot set limits. It *does* mean that you set limits, and enforce them, while still respecting your children. This dual approach of kindness, with limit-setting, will enhance your children's moral development. The result is that parents feel safe to their children—even when children feel frustrated. The children feel cared for, not bullied. Children understand that there are consequences for their misbehavior, but they have not been scared or treated disrespectfully in the process. Research consistently shows that children with secure attachments have better mental health and happier relationships.[9,10]

In summary:

- Children with secure attachments are more resilient when they hit life's stresses. They cope better and use help from others with more ease.

- Secure attachments predict better recovery after trauma or grief.

- Parents who have not had a secure attachment themselves are still able to form a secure attachment to their children if they value the qualities and mindset of secure attachment.

9   Sroufe, L.A., Egeland, B., Carlson, E., and Collins, W.A. (2005) *The Development of the Person: The Minnesota Study of Risk and Adaptation from Birth to Adulthood*, pp.286–304. New York: Guilford Press.
10 Berlin, L., Zeanah, C., and Lieberman, A. (2008) "Chapter 31: Prevention and Intervention Programs for Supporting Early Attachment Security." In J. Cassidy and P. Shaver (eds) *Handbook of Attachment* (2nd ed.), pp.745–761. New York: Guilford Press.

- No matter what children have lived through, or will live through, secure attachments help children to become more resilient adults.

- Attachments that are secure will help keep children's cortisol levels in a desirable range (cortisol measures stress).

- Secure attachment to a parent helps children to learn better and to bond to their teachers later on in childhood and into the teen years.

- The benefits of secure attachments continue in future generations as children attach to their children.

A check-list for attachment is listed in the Appendix. This check-list is extracted from a bonding and attachment assessment. Parents may enjoy noticing their progress towards patterns of security and away from patterns that are insecure and disorganized. Especially when children have come to parents past the newborn stage, it is to be expected that the patterns of security will take some time for both parents and children. Extra help for parents whose children are struggling with attachment may be found in the book, *Attaching in Adoption: Practical Tools for Today's Parents* (Gray 2012b).

Chapter 2

Parents and Attachment

Put Your Oxygen Mask on First

Parent's balance and children's security

What qualities describe you as a parent as you form secure attachments with your children?

> *Loving*
>
> *Nurturing*
>
> *Strong*
>
> *Sensitive*
>
> *Kind*
>
> *Stable*
>
> *Authoritative (Wise)*
>
> *Dependable*

As you parent, your children are more likely to develop into stable people, with empathy and self-control as character traits, when you show the traits above.

> *Anxious*
>
> *Depressed*
>
> *Chaotic*
>
> *Scary*
>
> *Weak*
>
> *Authoritarian (Overbearing)*

All of these are qualities that describe parents who will be least successful in forming secure attachments. If you find yourself on this list, then your relationships with your children will by marked by anxiety and/or avoidance, fears and/or role reversals. (By role reversals we refer to the way in which children meet their parents' needs, taking care of their parents emotionally and sometimes physically. This pressure to meet the needs of adults emotionally distorts children's development.)

As parents, we all have times of self-reflection during which we understand the need to care for ourselves in order to raise an emotionally healthy child. And, if you were raised in a healthy home with good boundaries, it will "feel right" when you are balancing caring for yourself and your child. While no parent wants to imitate the exact pattern of their parents, if you have secure attachments in your past, then you have an internal compass. The balance seems to come naturally when setting boundaries, responding to your children, and keeping back some time for self-care.

Parents who were not so lucky in their growing-up years will not have this compass, or natural sense of balance, to guide them. But, the beauty of doing your parenting well is that *your children* will have a compass when it is their turn to parent. This book is written to include those of you raised in tough families, or for those of you whose parenting is complicated due to upsets in your children's early development.

Mature parents are able temporarily to put children's needs above their own. However, this does not mean that you never get to prioritize yourself. You may want to think of deferring needs rather than denying them. For example, Lucia, aged three, spills cereal down the front of herself and into her mother's lap, while pouring the cereal and milk herself. Her mother will take a few minutes to change Lucia. The mother moves on to her own shower—even if Lucia protests that she would rather that her mother stays to eat with her.

I encourage parents to set a pattern early that they will take some time for their own basic needs—not in an insensitive manner, but in one that is sensitive to both parent and child. Emma is an example of a daughter whose mother needed to care for herself.

I asked eight-year-old Emma to wait in my waiting room (supervised by a kind receptionist) for ten minutes while I spoke to her parent. The single, adoptive mother needed a little time to problem-solve with me. Emma's mother had died when Emma was three, giving her reason to cling and protest at separation. But after four years with her adoptive mother, Emma remained anxious and controlling, sulking, weeping, and grabbing at her adoptive mother. I gave Emma my watch so that she could track the time. We started with three minutes of waiting, moving to 15 minutes. We comforted Emma, were sensitive to her feelings, but pointed out her mother's needs. Over eight sessions Emma de-sensitized to her wait. She became aware and considerate of her mother's need to talk to an adult without "all eyes on Emma." This became a template that her mother used in other areas of Emma's life.

Emma's distress at the time of the adoption made it difficult for her mother to set boundaries beyond those necessary for school and work. The rest of the time, Emma's extreme moods controlled their lives. Emma's mother was tired and lonely. A pattern of self-care, right from the beginning, would have included time for the mother to shower alone, sleep in her own bed (her dream), and speak to other adults. Trying to establish these patterns, after four years of Emma's rule, was challenging.

When children have come from harsh backgrounds, or if you have had your own experiences of abandonment or insensitivity, it can be hard to think when feelings are so high. Sometimes you may like to ask yourself, "Is this action a *reasonable* action to take?"

Reasonable self-care includes:

- caring for your physical self (daily shower or bath, exercise, haircuts, regular doctor and dentist appointments, etc.)

- making a living, and living on your income (regular work attendance, checking account is in the black and not in the red)

- time with supportive friends and relatives

- cleaning and laundry done without chaos

- meal preparation and grocery shopping is smooth

- romantic time (sex)

- sleeping seven or eight hours a night.

Most people have an adjustment period in which some of the areas above become a problem when they have a baby or child added to the family. But it is important to balance things again so that you feel a sense of order in your daily routines. That is part of the "compass" mentioned earlier.

Maintaining balance when children do not concur

Teaching children that you will maintain order, without crises or extreme emotion, is best done through your actions and behavior. Talking is not as helpful as living a balanced life. Some children will protest when you divert attention to the tasks or needs listed in the section above. Children really do not see the point! After all, the super Lego set is surely a higher priority than grocery money. And, why do those beds need to be made? We will just sleep in them tonight!

A helpful approach to the daily household tasks starts with encouraging children to participate in a playful manner. For example, my mother used to cover me with the fresh sheets when changing the bed linen. She pretended not to know what caused the long bump in the bed (my skinny body). Changing the sheets in my family took a little longer, but it was fun. Later, I learned to hold the other end of the sheets or tablecloths when folding linens. We would laugh when our ends met when folding large items. We told jokes as we folded large mounds of laundry. The attitude was that the tasks were neutral to fun when done together.

Similarly, when my children were young, if we accumulated too many "lonely socks," I had a "sock hunt." I paid money for every pair of socks we reunited. (Socks of one child were always ending up in the drawers of the others.) After the hunt we went shopping, and the children were allowed to spend some of the money from the sock hunt.

These are memories that teach children that household tasks, done together, can be fun and a necessary part of life. Introducing children to household tasks in an imaginative or fun manner will set the stage for a positive approach. Rather than blustering and shaming children when they do not regard parents' or household needs, parents simply behave in a balanced manner. For example, in the conversation below, James is asking to leave for football practice when there is a full dishwasher and a sink of dirty dishes. His parent does not want to come home and have to prepare dinner amidst a mess. The mother says:

> I can see how much you want to be early for your team's practice. I need to empty the dishwasher before we go. We can still be a little early if you help by putting all of the cutlery away. I wonder if I can finish putting away the plates and glasses before you finish with the cutlery? If I finish first, you'll feed the dog. If you finish first, I will.

Competitive children will jump right in. This works a bit better than being the parent who gets caught in an argument over whether or not the task is important. In the example, the parent is sensitive, playful, and hard to engage in an argument.

When we, as parents, begin to argue, we are not authoritative. We have conveyed that our children's views on the running of the household should hold sway over us. Sensitive parents listen to their children, but maintain the responsibility for the overall stability of the home and the family. This is different from when children approach us, asking for an alteration in a schedule or task. For example, a teen who asks to trade a cleaning job for a cooking one. Or a child who asks to trade morning jobs for after-school jobs. These are good ideas to try out.

Shaming children when we feel shame ourselves

Sometimes we feel guilty about saying "no" to children—especially when the "no" has to do with protecting our own needs or interests. We attempt to provide a justification that our children will understand. In situations where children do not agree, parents may move into long explanations of the parent's suffering, or the legitimacy of their needs. This shames children. Shaming children simply makes them feel bad about themselves and irritated with their parents. Covertly, children feel that their parents are inept at running the household. If parents are in charge and things are still so poorly run, then parents cannot be competent.

Parents who are feeling "ill-used" need to set limits, not place their children in the position of feeling responsible for the problem. All of us as parents will visit "guilt and shame land" during our children's growing-up years. But we try not to be residents!

Self-care includes putting our needs on the list of family resource essentials. Some parents give away their time for self-care. Then they complain about being a martyr. But a human response is to feel uncomfortable around these people. We end up feeling resentful because they control us through shame. For example:

> Moriah, with four children, complained that her older boys, aged 17 and 19 years old, would rarely help her with her young daughters, who had severe ADHD. Moriah described herself as constantly exhausted. Her husband worked overtime to meet the needs of the family. She asked for help from friends, who tended to help in a short-term manner and then fall away. Relatives seemed to be fleeting in their commitments. It turned out that any time that people did pitch in, Moriah simply took on more tasks.
>
> When Moriah's younger children were in preschool, rather than using the time for self-care, she volunteered to organize the school fundraiser. When a foreign exchange student needed housing and transportation, she volunteered the family home and provided the driving. Moriah ran a food bank out of the family garage. She described herself as lonely, with few friends and no sleep. She was a "grouch" according to her sons. Healthy people kept a distance from her, feeling that her lack of boundaries made helping her an endless proposition. Her sons were waiting to finish school and leave home.
>
> Moriah's husband said: "I do all that I can. When I ask her to cut back, she gets angry. I often wonder what our daughters would be like in a family that was organized and happy. Would they have such severe ADHD if our house didn't look like a storehouse?"
>
> Moriah's early life taught her that meeting the needs of others helped her to get her own needs met. She had been an energetic daughter of a needy single parent, who complained constantly. Moriah said: "Now I am just like my mother. I keep trying to get my kids to help me, like I helped my mother. Why don't they? They want me to reel my life back so that it is manageable. I don't seem to know how to do that. I'm in crisis mode all of the time."

A better alternative to meeting others' needs in order to get your own needs met is to stick up for yourself. This can be trickier than it seems if you are parenting needy children. You will receive signals and behavior from your children prompting you to give more because your children feel needy. You will need to be simultaneously mindful of your own needs and those of your children, balancing both. Austin, in the vignette below, was giving his mother cues that he needed her help:

> Janine's baby, Austin, was a "premie," born three months early. Finally, Austin was home and their family could get back to normal! But Janine found that she was getting up 10–15 times per night. Her husband had used all of his family leave when Austin was in the hospital. He got up once nightly, but slept through all of the wailing after that. He needed to keep his job now that Janine was no longer working.
>
> When Austin was born three months before, Janine's family came over with dinners. But now everyone seemed to think that life was back to normal. Austin was a fussy baby. Janine had been warned by the hospital that he would be irritable, but somehow had not thought that she would need help. She had been focused on getting him home. By the third day of little sleep, with Austin's crying approaching the two-hour mark, Janine was frantic. She found herself chanting, "I can't take it anymore." She found a pair of ear plugs so that she could mute Austin and think. Her first realization was that she smelled bad. Wandering into the bathroom, she assessed the woman looking back at her in the mirror. She looked like a raccoon with bad hair!
>
> Janine spent a half-hour showering, putting on clean clothes, breathing deeply, calming herself, eating some yogurt, and then finding music for the home. Austin had fallen asleep. She used the brief reprieve to call her dad—the calmest person she knew. He promised to take a half-day off work the following day, just to come and be with her.
>
> As Austin began to fuss again, Janine knew that she'd feed him and then escape the apartment. Just having a plan helped. She got Austin in the stroller and headed outside. Even though he cried off and on, Janine no longer felt trapped. While Austin was still not able to be in crowds until his immune system improved, they could at least walk in the park. As Janine calmed down, Austin seemed to do a little better, catching her better mood. When Janine's

husband came home from work, she was so pleased to have something positive to share. She felt like she was managing. He took over for the next few hours so that Janine could get some sleep.

In the vignette above, the time that Janine spent on herself moved her out of a crisis state. *When parents feel frantic, it is a danger sign that should be heeded.* Retreating for a short time to calm down, to reach out for help, or to make a plan will decrease the risk in the parenting situation. As Janine was better balanced, she helped little Austin to feel better balanced. Her slower, calm rhythms helped him to calm, even though his systems were still fragile.

Boundaries with time and attention

Our children need and deserve to be our highest priority. That is so easy to say and so tricky to do! Clear markers help parents to establish and maintain limits on their time and focus.

One of the best gifts that you can give yourself is a balanced schedule. Basic to best care for your children is best care for yourself. Being relaxed and emotionally present are rewards in themselves. *But they are necessities when attaching securely.*

When people are preoccupied or multitasking, even if they are physically present, they are not emotionally present. Their minds are elsewhere. Children will respond by being fussier or distant. Often they will do both.

Children, especially very young ones, are relying on a steady stream of cues or signals from parents to keep them on an even emotional keel. As parents become more distracted or harried, children become confused or irritable. This results in parents and children looking even more chaotic. Voices are raised, items are dropped or misplaced, communication suffers, and chaos builds.

We live in a culture of busyness. When asked how we are doing, a typical response is, "busy." The message is that this is uncomfortable, but normal. While it is typical, it is not normal or healthy for parents and children.

Parents will need to be strong in defending time with their children. The many good things to do in life can accumulate as the enemy of the best. Often we are trained to think of our worth as the sum of what we did or accomplished during the day.

Take a moment to think about the way that you will feel saying to yourself: "I spent time forming a secure attachment with my child. I showed my child the importance of relationships. Specifically, I showed him how important he was to me." Now contrast that with your saying, "I finished two more items on my to-do list." It simply does not compare.

> A parent had her nine-year-old and his friend in the back seat of the car. She heard him say: "My mother makes a lot of money every hour she works. But she would rather come home early four days a week to spend time with me." Children are constantly learning lessons about attachment, whether or not we want them to.
>
> Another 16-year-old said: "My nannies were the ones who heard about my days at school. My parents loved me, but they were always working. I will not raise my children like they raised me." She looked small and forlorn. I sadly reflected not only on the careers of both parents, but on their volunteerism and hobbies. They simply did not set necessary boundaries. Neither parent was aware of the loneliness in their daughter's eyes. They had undermined her self-esteem. Their articulate rationalizations were just that—rationalizations rather than boundaries.

I encourage parents to protect times simply to play with and enjoy their children.

> One parent, a manager in her firm, said: "I realized that I care for my children, but never take time to play with them or actually enjoy them. When I watched you playing with my daughter, and then waiting until she got her thoughts together, I thought, 'Deborah Gray could speed up and finish this 60-minute session in 40 minutes instead of one hour.' Then I realized what the problem was. I'm acting like my time with my children is a work project. I try to speed through our time together. We don't set aside time to play or to talk. When my daughter doesn't remember something, or has trouble putting her thoughts into words, I speak for her and move on. I need to let her express herself and practice communicating."

Parents may begin blaming others—children, family members, and society in general—when overwhelmed and overly busy. Changing others may be part of the solution, but it is a more direct approach to change in ourselves the things that we can change.

> Leah was in grief after her mother passed on. She was parenting two children who were adopted after neglect. While the family was doing relatively well, the children had some special issues from their background. Leah and her husband had been careful with their finances so that they did not have to use childcare. As a result, one of the parents was always available before and after school with the children. Leah said: "I'm constantly getting requests to volunteer. I do not even have my mother's clothes sorted out yet. My children hardly saw me for the last six months as I spent time with my mother.
>
> "They are acting out, since loss brings up issues for them. My daughter asked, 'Will we have another mother if you die?' What do I tell people who ask for my help? I don't really want to share my children's personal issues. I get angry at other people for asking for my time so casually, and angry at my children for being so needy."
>
> Leah listed her priorities. She found that she was cutting out her self-care to meet the needs of others. When she looked at the list of her priorities, she found it easier to say "no." She simply wrote a polite note saying that she had prior commitments.

You and your children are commitments which should not be short changed. Leah had a couple of rather persuasive friends who were not attuned to her personal situation. Leah needed to stop trying to please them at the expense of herself or her family. When she did so, she operated within limits so that she felt peaceful again. In Leah's case, her mother's death meant that she needed more quiet time to process her thoughts. Until she gave herself the time she needed, she felt overwhelmed, resenting others for not noticing her grief.

Boundaries and community

Creating community is important for us all. When we begin parenting, it usually results in shifting the people in your life—letting supportive people in and omitting those whose needs compete with your children's needs. Many of our friends shift with us as we move into parenting mode, but most parents find that their circles change because of the tasks of parenting. Similarly, our circles shift once again if we are parenting children with special needs. Some of our friends and family will make the transition in supporting our family, some we will see less often.

When forming attachments you can include supportive others who can take a turn in some of the caregiving. This can come via grandparent and relative help, or through friends. One goal is to allow you some time for a break. Another is to include your child in the process of making friends with other families or relatives. It is great to have children see you with friends, picking up on the processes of friendship. These connections help children to understand the value of community.

Children who have experience with family friends will automatically feel more capable in social situations. They will already have connections with people outside of the family or school. Family friends build esteem in the whole family. As children move into teen years, a friend may act as a mentor. Having involved adult friends, who are positive role models, shows up as an important factor in research that looks at teen well-being.[1]

An exception to this rule is in the earliest stages of adjustment, with children newly placed for adoption, when adoptive parents will want to do almost all of the caregiving. However, they will certainly want to move to the model of having other supportive adults to help them share some of the load after the initial transition period.

The earlier paragraphs deal primarily with including people in your life and your child's life. Sometimes the rub comes when we have to work to exclude others or their requests. In parenting there are watershed incidents, warning us to change course. The example below is one. Either Amber changes, taking care of herself by setting boundaries, or else she passes on dysfunction to the next generation.

Amber said to me: "I have always taken care of everyone in my family—starting with my dad. At ten years old I had to call the bars to tell the bartender to send him home. I would say to

---

1   Rick, E. and Tricker, R. (2003) "Resiliency-Based Research and Adolescent Health Behaviors." *Prevention Researcher,* 10(1): 1–14.

the bartender, 'Mom and my baby sister are crying, send Dad home.' Now I am parenting. We finally adopted a little girl, and instead of enjoying it, I am a mess. My mother and sister still call all of the time. My daughter starts hitting me when I am on the phone with them. My husband says that I sound unbalanced when I'm on the phone. I know that my anxiety from the phone calls is leaking onto my daughter. It makes her upset and angry. I thought that after I adopted my daughter, my family would know that I needed to put her first!"

Amber chose to have a talk with her mother, who agreed to stop calling her and to get professional counseling. Amber's mother volunteered to provide childcare on Saturday evenings so that Amber could have date nights with her husband.

"I am kicking myself that I endured this for so long," Amber said. I do not answer the phone or check messages from the time I get home from work until my daughter goes down. That way, if my family calls, I am not interrupting my time with our daughter. Now that I don't pick up the phone, it turns out that they just go on to the next person. I guess I wasn't as crucial as I thought."

Making certain that we are part of healthy relationships is a critical part of parenting. Most of us tolerate some unhealthy situations, and may even be the source of much of the problem. Parenting is a wonderful time to ask a little more of ourselves in setting good boundaries that respect us and others around us.

Boundaries—deciding on time for yourself

When your children are forming attachments with you, and you are trying to be especially attuned to them, you are actually expending a great deal of emotional energy. You will do best if you can have breaks. Enjoying a hobby, talking walks, going to movies, joining a parent support group, journaling, praying or meditating, and maintaining friendships are all important ways to make time for your well-being. A friend of mine said:

I have successfully raised three children, worked, and supported my husband. But, I think that I lost myself for a while. My adult children do not want to imitate me. I poured myself out for my family, and my daughters pity me.

I suggest that you think of the type of self-care that you would like your children to have someday. Give that to yourself, modeling respect for yourself.

In that same vein, it is important to have some time that is simply devoted to keeping track of yourself. Those are chunks of time that allow you some deeper thought, answering questions for yourself, such as: "How am I doing? Is my life meaningful? Do I need to make some life changes? What priorities need to shift?" This does not have to be dislocating to everyone else. Typically, people can take 5–20 hours a month, just for themselves, feeling that they are doing well with that much time off when their children are young. Some people need a little time to themselves daily, others like chunks of time weekly or monthly.

Most parents feel more authentically "present" with themselves and their families when they have time to themselves. Being "present" means that they are fully engaged and emotionally connected with what is occurring. If we do not take breaks, we tend to drift off, being physically but not emotionally present. Our minds are looking for ways to shut off the flow of new information until we make sense of the current information. We have to process, or think about, new information in order to understand the meaning of the information and to mentally categorize it. When we do not have private, quiet time, it is hard to process information as it comes in. The "pile up" of unprocessed information will cause people to feel confused, or as if they are playing a role. If this is happening to you, then having quiet time will begin to remedy this situation, so that you feel like you are living your own life again.

Parents lead the dance of attachment

Even if you are sensitive and capable, yours may not be the first parenting experience that your child has had. You may be parenting after your child has had an emotionally distant parent, an emotionally unstable parent, a high-stress custody situation, or a series of foster homes. Your child may expect that adults will do a poor job in meeting their needs. Children who have had these experiences usually give inconsistent messages about their needs. They may be hard for you to soothe, may not believe that you are coming when they call to you, and may push away when you reach out to snuggle them. They may cling too tightly when you hold them, or else slip right through your arms, not clinging at all. Children are not consciously trying to reject their parents, but have an automatic response of trying to shield themselves from hurt. It can feel like rejection to parents who are on the receiving end, as in the example below.

> An 11-year-old girl was in my office with her adoptive mother, Carrie, working on their relationship. "I wish that she would show me some affection," said Carrie. "She doesn't act like I'm worth much."
>
> The daughter acted confused. "I love you," she insisted.
>
> "You don't hug me like you love me," said Carrie.
>
> I asked the daughter to show how she and her mother hugged. The girl hugged her mother in a tentative manner—as if Carrie might be contagious.
>
> When I showed the child how to "hug back," she said, "It feels different—weird." Her reaction made perfect sense, given her background of abuse and neglect prior to adoption. She tried over the next weeks to give firmer and more enthusiastic hugs. She said that it began feeling normal instead of weird.
>
> Carrie said: "I never stopped showing her love, even when she did not respond in a loving manner. I'm finally getting the response that lets me know how much she cares. She has been my daughter for three years. But I really feel connected to her now."

The key to Carrie's success was her ability to show her daughter what Carrie knew about love, or attachment. She stayed positive, consistent, and nurturing. She nurtured through her daughter's inconsistent responses. Finally, her daughter was able to respond, with some help, in a reciprocal manner. As her attachment security improved, the girl became very kind to her brother, which was an enormous change from the time of placement. She learned how to be sensitive to the needs of others through her attachment relationship with Carrie.

The effect on parents when children respond inconsistently is to want to push away as well. They can become caught in a dilemma—try harder or give up. Instead, parents should maintain a calm, consistent, positive, and warm attitude towards a child. The parent leads the dance in these families, showing the child the positive steps towards attachment.

Attachment, mirror neurons, and magical brains

When we pat a baby on the back, how do they know how to pat us back? Of course, it seems like common sense that they have observed the pat, experienced it, and are patting back. In fact, without having been taught, they are using what are called "mirror neurons." These allow our brains to watch and repeat the actions of another. How this works is interesting. When we are watching, our brains are "firing up" the motor (movement) parts of our brains as if we are doing the same activities. Later, we have the pattern for these activities laid down neurologically. We "fire up" the same brain pathway, this time doing the activity, not just watching it.

Not only do we have these patterns in the motor areas of the brain, but we have them in the emotional centers of our brains. That is why we can perceive that someone likes us, or is interested in us, even if we have just met them. While we are not always completely accurate, we still rely heavily on this information that is conveyed from one person to another without our even having to speak to one another.

When parenting, we want our children to use their mirror neurons, picking up positive messages from us rather than negative ones. When we are tired or distracted, we will want to exhale deeply, getting rid of negative thoughts, then take a cleansing breath and think some helpful thoughts. Those thoughts will actually change our feelings and our neural firing patterns.

For example, after my commute home after work I used to breathe deeply, saying: "How fortunate I am to have a family to come home to! This is what I always wanted in life—a family to love and care for." I would reflect on this as I sat in the car for a minute. Then, I was able to greet my family with love and full attention. It was a *mindful* practice that allowed me to transition in the manner that I enjoyed. Because of mirror neurons, my children reflected back to me the expressions of gratitude and joy most of the time. Sometimes there were low moments, but they were a minority.

Of course, like many character changes, this practice came about because of failures. I moved into this practice because I was dissatisfied with my former practice of dragging my work and commute home with me. My family found my preoccupation and irritability contagious—even if I kept my words polite (which I did not always do). When I practiced mindful parenting, I could feel the mood in the room shift to one of joy, connection, and relaxation.

It only takes a few minutes to "reset" our grouchy or overwhelmed brains. Do some deep breathing, imagine yourself at the beach or in a forest, take a nice bath, smell a pleasing fragrance, do 100 jumping jacks, pray aloud, sing a song loudly and with passion... All of these are things that allow you to catch up with yourself. I suggest following this up with a "mission statement" about who you are and what you are about. For example: "My family is the most treasured part of my life. I will do my best to be present and engaged for this stage of my children's lives." A statement for a child with special need's might be: "I am glad that this is my child. I have the skills, love, and determination to meet this child's needs with the help of my community. I will open myself up to the experience."

These "big picture" descriptions help us to put things into perspective and to have more balanced brain patterns (neural firing patterns). Our children, who are looking to us as their touchstones for life, will respond in a more positive manner. Since their brain structures are developing in early childhood, we have the opportunity to shape these developing structures so that they lay down the wiring for positive, emotionally stable brains. Their more positive wiring will help children to perceive their worlds in a more positive manner. Your example will teach them the patterns of optimism.

Attachment when parents grieve

When parents have painful, unresolved grief, they have brain patterns unique to grief. Because of the way children's brains connect with their parents, children and infants experience some of these grief feelings as they become attached to their parents. Children are not able comfortably to feel these overwhelming and negative feelings. It actually interferes with the formation of a secure attachment. Children will shy away from their parents, alternating between fussy, controlling, or angry behavior.

Of course, it is not anyone's choice to join the ranks of the grief-stricken. We cannot control life, the timing of tragic instances or the death of our loved ones. However, we can plan to get help to process our grief. "Processing the grief" means that we receive the support and time that allow us to think about who we lost, and our feelings towards that person. We think about the significance of that person to us, our family, and how our loss affects our world view. We hold onto the memory of the lost person as a last step. The alternative, just pushing away the loss, requires a great deal of emotional effort. Inevitably the losses pop up anyway.

Some parents "pretend" to be bright and cheery when they are experiencing loss. Because of the way that the brain works, this is not successful. Children simply feel disoriented when parents are grief-stricken, have the brain patterns to prove it, and then grin. It is better to say: "I am sad right now because I am missing my mother. You are a great kid. This is not about you. I will be taking a little time to sort myself out today so that I feel better."

Support groups or professional counseling are indicated if parents are finding that unresolved grief keeps popping into their minds, or that they are becoming depressed because the grief has not been processed. Some people do not have access to either counseling or a support group. A friend of mine found that her way to process her grief from the losses of her adoptive mother and birthmother was through a weekly visit to an older woman, who simply talked with her about the losses and who treated her like a daughter.

More important than who supports our grief, is finding some support and time to process grief so that our brain patterns become resolved ones, rather than the overwhelmed brain patterns that are typical of all of us when we are in deep grief. That way our children are put into connection with our regulated (balanced) brain patterns. They can use their parent as a basis for their own emotional balance. They will be able to form a secure attachment.

Attachment and worrying parents

Some people tilt towards being natural worriers. They produce more "what if" worries than are warranted. They either generate the next generation of worriers, or they have children who tune their parents out. An anxious mother described her adult daughters. Two of them worried constantly. The other was so used to tuning out anxiety, that she did not include its warnings in her plans. She ended up touring an impoverished country alone, with little money, and no organizational back-up. She became hospitalized there. The goal for our children is to teach them a realistic appraisal of risk, with some back-up when going into situations of unavoidable risk.

Parents who are worriers should train themselves to develop two solutions or possible actions for every "watch out" statement. Those solutions and their stem worries are best edited mentally before being spoken. They should also calculate the amount of time spent on the worry. It should be limited to the probability that the adverse outcome might happen. For example, the probability of an outcome might be 1 percent. The time spent on the worry would be trimmed to meet a 1 percent chance.

Worriers decrease the joy of exploration, the amazement of being in such a fabulously interesting world. Anxiety leeches the joy of developing new relationships of all kinds. If you are a serial worrier, then using stress reduction skills should be part of your daily practice.

If you are the partner of a worrier, you, and eventually your children, may be drafted into the worry wars. That is, you will be expected to help to assure the worrier, reassure them, and then reassure them again. This can be a drag on your own mood. And, it takes a lot of time. Worse, over time it takes the worrier more and more reassurance in order to be calmed. I suggest that you tell the worrier that you will limit yourself to one reassuring answer, one helpful comment, when confronted with the list of worries. Otherwise you will become part of an obsessive habit. This message is given respectfully, kindly, and consistently.

Anxious people have brains that work differently. They need to learn to assess risk realistically, to use calming techniques, and to move on. Being part of a family that does not circulate around the person's anxiety actually helps the anxious person much more than a family member's long, careful listening and multiple reassurances. Children who are getting stuck in a worry loop seem to do very well with about ten professional therapy sessions, learning skills to deal with anxiety.

Attachment and trauma

Trauma's brain patterns are overwhelming to children, just as the grief patterns are. When children or infants are in close contact with traumatized parents, they turn away from the parents. Or, they go "still-faced." That is, they shut down emotional processing and try to go into an emotional freeze. This is not healthy for them. In fact, they are learning the brain patterns of dissociation. In dissociation, the person is present, but stops the normal integration of information that is coming from their outside world or inside themselves. Mentally, "the lights are on, but no one is home." Children feel disoriented and confused when they are with a parent who dissociates. They will not form a secure attachment with this person.

Of course, no one chooses to be a traumatized adult. But while it is not the parent's fault, it is their responsibility to care for themselves so that they are able to provide good care for their children.

Parents, who want to know whether trauma has influenced them to the degree that they are at-risk, may do a brief self-assessment using the following questions:

- Do the sounds, smells, or mental images of a traumatic event come into my mind daily or weekly, even though I do not want to be thinking of these events?

- Do I avoid places and situations that remind me of the trauma? Does the avoidance interfere with the typical routines of my family life?

- Do I have trouble keeping my moods steady?

- Do I feel as if other traumas are more likely to occur to me than to others, or that there might be omens that I need to pay attention to?

- Do I have nightmares that include some of the events of the trauma?

- Do I feel like I am an actor in a play, or that I am watching my life, rather than actually living?

- Do others seem to see obvious risks that I do not see? Or, do I seem to see many more risks than others do?

- Do I have physical symptoms that do not have a source? Do I hurt for no medical reason? Do I seem to be aging much faster than I should?

- Do I startle easily? Does my heart rate go up and does my breathing increase after something startles me, and does it stay up for some time?

All of these are symptoms of trauma. The good news is that the treatment for trauma has advanced wonderfully in the last decades. Refer to the resource list in the back of this book to begin the search to find help for yourself or your child.

Often, parents find that they thought themselves recovered from an early life trauma only to have it resurface when faced with a "trigger" (a mental reminder that reminds them of the trauma). For example, they might be reminded of the trauma when their child is the same age as they were when a trauma occurred. I mentioned day care to a woman who had been severely sexually abused. She thought that she had dealt with her trauma from sexual abuse until I mentioned finding child care for her daughter. The trauma was triggered at the thought of leaving her daughter outside her care or that of her husband and his family.

Parents may want to think ahead in a preventative manner, exploring what events could trigger a reaction in themselves or their spouse or partner. For example, children's screaming can trigger a parent's trauma reaction. Parents have found that eye movement de-sensitization and reprocessing (EMDR) is helpful when they have processed the meaning of the trauma and simply have a trigger left. Other parents have used exposure therapy, which includes telling their trauma story, with the thoughts and feelings put together, to a trauma therapist.

When people find themselves with trauma triggers or some of the symptoms listed earlier, mental health therapy is essential. Parents need to be able to provide consistent, safe-feeling care for their children. Even if their intention towards their children is sterling, trauma brain patterns will cause their children to react to them in a confused, disoriented, and often hostile manner.

Children with traumatized parents do not form secure attachments. Instead, they form a style of attachment that reflects the brain patterns of fear and avoidance in their parents' brains (disorganized attachment style). Sadly, the trauma not only impacts the parent but the next generation as well.

Because our brain's neural firing patterns (patterns of brain activity) cause similar firing patterns in our children, we actually create some of these trauma-influenced patterns in our children— even if they have not had the trauma. A series of research studies showed the impact of trauma on many of the children of people who survived Hitler's concentration camps. The children were impacted even though they had never experienced trauma. They had "downloaded" some of their parent's brain patterns. When children turn away from traumatized parents, it is their attempt to protect themselves and their development. Of course, this feels very confusing for both parents and children.

If you are a parent with unresolved trauma, you owe it to yourself and your child to get treatment. When parents have a young family, they are often reluctant to divert time or resources into their own mental health. This is a gentle reminder that it is important to make the connection between our own mental health, as parents, and our children's mental health and happiness. Parents who take care of themselves have an opportunity to shape their children's development for the better. It is an unselfish, courageous act to get therapy for trauma.

Attachment and friends

Friends help us all to put our lives into a context that makes sense. We all need friends to have fun with and spend time with. When tough times come, they care about us. Parenting can include some horrible days. Just in talking about the horrible day with our friends, we move from the gloom of our "horrible day" to laughing about it. For example:

> One of my children scaled the cupboards to reach the top shelf where the multi-pack of green sugarless gum was kept. She chewed wads of gum and then dotted her body. It stuck like glue. Large dollops ended up in her waist-length hair, and then stuck to the tub during clean-up. I used peanut butter (chunky was what was at hand) to break down the gum globs. Friends arrived in the midst of the clean-up, while my husband was at the store buying more peanut butter (creamy, by request). My frustration was mirrored back to me as hilarity. They asked if we were having peanut butter sandwiches. They came up with lame excuses to view our tub. They noted, sadly, that we had only chunky-style peanut butter as our option. They admired the color combination— green gum and pink tutu—that my daughter was rocking. It got hard to take the situation so seriously.

We need that balance. We also need someone who cares about our well-being, and not just our children's. Taking care of ourselves includes some time with friends or time as part of groups of parents and children together.

Within a short time of parenting, parents realize that parenting is idealized by society. Yes, it is absolutely wonderful to spend time with children, and it is absolutely awful at times. The awful tends to come when we can never get a moment for ourselves, when the children are sick and cranky, and when we are trying to do tasks that require our children to behave in a certain manner, and they simply will not or cannot behave. And there are the occasional mega messes that can seem epic at the time.

Friends help us to recover our sense of self and perspective. They show sympathy, care about our well-being, and laugh and cry with us. Your ability to form secure attachments is enhanced by friends who help you throughout your life.

Friends when your child has special needs

Parents of special needs children often struggle to find supportive friends.

> A parent whose youngest child had a brain injury said: "My friends used to welcome my older children. We were favorites for play dates. Now it's a quick 'hi' before they invite someone who is typically developing."
>
> The parent said: "We need to find other families who could relate to *all* of our members." They were able to do this through participation in the Special Olympics. It created an opportunity for their typically developing children to find friendships, as well as their child with special needs. They all attended events, enjoying the sense of inclusion.

Even within similar groups, some communities are more sensitive and affirming than others, as in the case of the Smythe family.

> The Smythe family moved to worship at another church, another denomination. They said quietly: "People accept our family there. The first week another girl asked my daughter to come sit beside her and with her family. The parents met our eyes and welcomed us. Someone actually thought and cared that we might be lonely. Of course we want to be included! Did our old parish really think that our daughter wanted to sit alone every week when all the other tween girls sat together? It broke our hearts. This new congregation is healing to us."

We all need to find places and people who allow us to relax and to expect acceptance. Otherwise, we become defensive and lonely. In busy lives, the essential needs of unhurried time with our families and our friends, our spiritual relationships, and time for self-reflection need to be high on our priority list. The more challenging our lives, the more we need to be mindful of keeping the priorities above.

Summary

In summary, your well-being will support the well-being of your child. Your steady, balanced brain will influence the actual brain development of your child. Part of being the best parent that you can be is taking good care of yourself. The outcome that all parents are reaching towards is raising children who connect with us and others, and who have compassion for others and themselves. We do this best by our daily example.

Chapter 3

Teaching Our Children Emotional Skills and Daily Responsibility

We all want to shape our children's behavior while still maintaining positive connections with our children. Sometimes it seems that it would be great if we could all focus on emotional connection, skipping limits or daily routines. Instead, by using our close connections with our children, we are able to help them with the skills that they need to get along with others and to take care of their responsibilities.

In childhood we begin to expect children to take on responsibilities. Our expectations may frustrate our children, which gives them the chance to develop qualities of calming, compromise, caring, and responsibility. We use our relationship to help them to develop these qualities.

In this chapter we will look at emotional skills and daily responsibilities.

Shaping behavior and enforcing limits will be most successful if the overall parenting plan is solid. The atmosphere in the home is essential: respect for ourselves and our children. This chapter looks at some of the essential "self-skills," or skills we have within ourselves, such as calming, thinking of others' points of view, taking a perspective, and compromise.

Chapter 4 will look at methods of helping children who are not as strong in skills of calming, remembering, organizing, flexibility, and impulse control. To the degree that we help our children in these areas, we will need to use fewer consequences. We will move on to limit-enforcing in Chapter 5, discussing consequences, or "carrots and sticks." "Consequences," in the parenting context, means the thing that will happen if our children do or do not comply.

Teaching our children calming and self-control

"Calm down!" When we say that, we need to think: Does our child know how to calm yet? Have we taught them?

Any time that we are thinking about reasonable consequences for behavior, we have to think about the capacities that children actually have developed. We want to work within the window of their abilities, stretching those abilities. For example, if a child is able to calm down while waiting in line in their primary school, we can build on that accomplishment. If they can wait calmly three times a day at school, can they work on staying calm in the grocery store line? I like to mention the goal, posing it as a challenge. For example, "My challenge for you is to calm yourself for a whole day, without yelling at your sister." Throwing in a reward is always fun.

When children do not know how to calm down, we want to stay with them, coaching them. The younger children are (measured not only by their years, but their emotional age), the more we, as parents, will expect to help them in calming.

Infants and toddlers rely on parents to teach them to calm:

- through the parents' calming voice tones

- by reducing the amount of stimulation for an overstimulated child (noise, movement, lights, trips outside the home)

- by using comforting or encouraging body positions (holding a child, standing beside a child and encouraging a child to approach something new that makes them wary)

- by distracting children and helping them to focus on something else

- by giving sensitive attention that allows children to feel that they are understood.

As parents repeat these calming, soothing, and distracting activities, children gradually develop the brain patterns to calm down. For many children, these patterns are developed without much effort. Parents both model them and teach them in typical parenting.

By four years of age, most children are learning enough about calming themselves that they are able to enjoy playing with other children, rather than just beside them. They still may hit. As they approach five years of age, the hitting has largely disappeared. Not only can they calm themselves, but they are keeping themselves in a play situation so that they can include the needs and interests of a play partner.

Some of you may be like parents who have said to me:

No one *ever* taught my child to calm! What about my six-year-old? She has been in my home for six months. I was told to use time out or consequences for a child of her age. She gets so upset! I have been leaving her alone to scream it out. She does eventually stop yelling, but it takes an hour.

If you are the new primary parents of a child, whether due to custody changes, foster care, or adoption, you are invited to be detectives. Think of your child's history. Was there a previous parent figure in your child's life who was a well-balanced, emotionally attuned (emotionally empathic and balanced) individual? *Do you have any evidence that your child has learned the ability to calm?* When the answer is "no," parents will need to teach children to calm as they would a much younger child. The list on page 84 is for you, even if your child is no longer a toddler.

Some parents find it chilling, but oddly confirming, to realize that they are the first to help their child to learn to calm. It is chilling to think of a child who has been left alone in their own emotional and physical misery. It is chilling to think of the age of their child, and how the work on emotional regulation (emotional balance) is just beginning. The confirming part is that the blow-ups, melt-downs, and rages are not personal. Their child is not "out to get them." Their child is not deliberately sending the family into turmoil.

Many adopted children have scant individual care prior to adoption, especially if adopted from an orphanage. Parents may have children who seem to calm by "shutting down," or "going into the zone," as parents describe it. In other words, children shut down emotionally. These children have not had anyone to buffer them from distress in the neglectful setting. Their wait for food, attention, and care exceeded/surpassed their threshold of emotional and/or physical distress. They have learned that yelling, protesting, or crying does no good. They may have been punished or separated from other children for their loud protest. So, they shut down. This is a dissociative pattern—a sign of trauma. (Dissociation allows people to experience a temporary distance from what is occurring in the present. It is a sign of extreme distress.)

For these children, even if they are older, it is a good idea to help them to learn how to calm rather than use time out or consequences after the problem. All of us as parents want to build a calming and coping pattern rather than a shut-down. Normally parents want their children to turn to them for help. In this situation, we are simply moving the time-frame back to teach older children the calming that they optimally would have had as younger children. Rachel's example below shows what this would look like in a younger child.

Rachel is three years old. She has a custodial arrangement that includes splitting time with each parent. She has left her father's home after spending the weekend with him. Her mother has picked her up in the family van. On the way home, Rachel says that she is hungry. Mom says, "Almost home." Rachel begins to fuss. Mom says: "Almost home, sweetie. Just hold on a little longer." Mom begins to breathe out audibly. She sings a little soothing song.

After pulling into the driveway, she takes Rachel out of the car seat. She holds Rachel against her. She pats her back, breathes deeply, and calms Rachel—who cries for about five minutes. They walk together inside the house. Rachel is getting back into balance with her mother. Mom puts a few things away, with Rachel clinging to her, and then holds Rachel on her lap. She puts some cereal in a bowl, without milk, and reads to Rachel, who slowly eats the cereal as finger food. Then, they move into a bedtime routine.

Later, Dad emails: "Rachel didn't eat dinner. She seemed to have a rough time with our transition." Mom thinks carefully about how to resolve the problem, before she replies, in order to help Rachel next time.

Contrast this approach with the following example, where we have the same events, but Mom is not available to help Rachel emotionally.

> Rachel is on her way home. She begins to fuss, saying that she is hungry. Mom says. "Didn't your Dad feed you?" Mom gets angry and begins to mutter. Rachel begins to howl. Mom cries out to the universe, "How am I supposed to drive when she's like this? What did I ever do to deserve this?" Rachel is in misery.
>
> When they get into the driveway, Mom pulls Rachel out of the car seat in grim silence. She marches both of them into the house, sitting Rachel at the table with a bowl of cereal with milk. "That's all I've got," she says. "Your Dad was supposed to feed you." Rachel knocks the cereal on the floor. Mom puts her in time out. When she does not stay, Mom dumps her into bed without a bedtime ritual. Rachel cries herself to sleep.
>
> Dad emails, but Mom deletes the message in frustration.

This is an example of a child who needs her parent in order to calm.

When teaching children to calm, it helps to hold them close to us. This can be a posture of low and beside, in front, or behind them. Our hands are gentle, and our voice tones soothing. Figures 3.1(a) and 3.1(b) illustrate this.

Figure 3.1(a): Parent with child, calming child.

Figure 3.1(b): Parent with child, calming irritable child.

The first step in teaching our children to calm is to provide our physical presence. Through our presence we teach children that they are not alone in their distress. They do not have to shriek or destroy things to get our attention.

Parents who speak in a soothing way, just behind children's ears, help children to hear, and later recall, their parent's soothing voice (see Figures 3.2(a) and 3.2(b)). Over time those soothing voice tones and the calming patterns of their parent's breathing become embedded in children's own brain patterns.

Figure 3.2(a): Parent behind child, calming child.

Figure 3.2(b): Parent behind child, calming busy child.

Take a moment to reflect on what you remember as the soothing tones of your parents from your childhood. If your parents were usually kind and caring, the voice tones are kind and soothing. The words are often very simple: "It's OK. We love you. We are here."

Similarly, notice your own mental self-talk (the words that you say in your head, or even out loud if no one is listening). What do you say to yourself when you are upset? What calms and soothes you so that you are able to calm yourself, pull yourself together, and move on? Who taught you to calm, and what did they say? Perhaps you would like to call or visit your parents or grandparents to find out the simple words that they said. Occasionally, these turn out not to be words, but little songs or lullabies. For example, my mother's soothing was often in the form of a little song, since she is a musician. My father used simple three-word sentences.

Sometimes people will note, with despair, that they never had models. Now is a good time to create one for yourself, giving a gift both to yourself and your child as you develop some soothing self-talk. Borrow some nice words from friends who were lucky enough to have nurturing parents. Write the words down, memorize them, and use them for yourself and your child. You are both worth kind words and encouragement.

Some parents had harsh words said to them. They were scared into silence. Obviously, this is something you do not want to pass on. A parent told me that she was afraid to fall apart as a child. Her dad, a career soldier, would get harsh. "I know he meant well. He loved me," she said. "When I am frustrated with my son I catch myself thinking and even repeating my dad's rough words. He was adopted after abuse, so I am sure that it is even worse for him when I'm saying mean things." Through practice, she eventually managed to soothe her son, rather than passing on her father's words or yelling in his face. "Kinder words help me, too," she said. "I've stopped yelling at myself when I have problems. I let myself get sad instead of angry."

Calming through breathing

One of the most effective ways to calm at any age is to slow our breathing. We use the term *belly breathing* for children, which is breathing so that they expand their bellies when they breathe in. (There is a little video listed in the resource section showing belly breathing.) So that they breathe deeply, we have them practice "breathing in through your nose out through your mouth." (Children with colds or congestion will need to use their mouths for both breathing in and out.)

Deep breathing slows the stress response, since slowing breathing slows our heart rates. With infants and very young children, parents can model this breathing for their children, slowing their breathing and using a calming voice in order to model for little ones. Standing in front of children, and getting low, causes children to want to practice with you some of the time.

I teach children (and their parents) to take three sets of three deep breaths in and out, for a total nine breaths. There is more emphasis on breathing out than breathing in. The breathing out, or blowing out, should take until the count of ten, at least. Older children and adults may get to the count of 20–25 when breathing out. I like to have stressed children practice this breathing several times a day at home. We simply set a timer to go off periodically through the day. It helps children to learn deep breathing as an automatic response if their parents model deep breathing during stressful times of the day.

Playful deep breathing for children

A more playful deep breathing technique is to have children pretend that their forefingers are candles. Ask them to blow out with a big breath—as if they are blowing out birthday candles. Then, compliment children on how hard they are blowing out!

When children have specific, troubling thoughts, I like to ask them to pretend to blow up a big balloon with their worries. Then they visualize letting the balloon drift away. Some children have several balloons that need to take flight before they feel calmer. I use actual balloons with children, as well. The anxious child turns into a fun-loving and relaxed child who chases balloons around the room. Parents can easily do this.

Give myself a hug or shake it out

Children may want quick options besides deep breathing. If people cross their arms in front of themselves, with their right hand squeezing their left shoulder, and their left hand squeezing their right shoulder, it looks like a hug (see Figures 3.3(a) and 3.3(b)). We call that "giving yourself a hug." This squeeze helps to calm children. It also prevents them from striking out with their hands. After the strong squeeze, children will relax and breathe deeply. It works with adults, as well.

Figure 3.3(a): Give myself a hug.

Figure 3.3(b): Give myself a hug.

Another technique starts with relaxing, not tensing. We ask kids to loosen their knees and shake out their arms and legs. They look like sports players or divers, loosening their muscles before an event. "Shake it out!" I'll say. "Shake it out, baby." The kids will grin at that. They like being like a sports figure. Again, this works well in releasing tension or anger. See Figure 3.4.

Figure 3.4: Shake it out.

Simple ways to help children's moods

When children are feeling strong, unpleasant feelings such as shame, loneliness, or anger, they often need physical ways to reduce the intensity of their feelings. Some of the favorites for children are:

- going for a brief walk or run
- kicking a soccer ball or football
- stretching
- petting a cat or dog
- getting a drink
- going to the bathroom
- taking a warm bath
- drawing
- riding a bike
- chewing gum
- getting a hug
- having a foot massage
- smelling a good fragrance
- doing jumping jacks
- running around the house ten times
- singing.

Try out several of these things with your child. You can come up with tried-and-true favorites for your children. Initially, it works best if parents are willing to do these activities with their children. Later they will find that their children become self-starting in choosing these natural mood changers, as in the example below.

Jim, a single parent who worked from home, would start the day with a cranky son. The morning routine was "a bear," in his terms. His son had attention issues and anxiety. Jim told me what the morning was like:

Morning on school days... First he fights me every step of the routine, since he's half asleep. We argue. He says that I'm mean and I don't like him. Then he cries that he feels scared of leaving me and that he's not ready for the day. By the time he leaves, I'm ready to have a stiff drink. That would be 8:30 in the morning.

We made a plan for some physical exercise. When any of us, as parents, are not sure what to do next, it is always a good idea to help the body first.

Jim began to walk and run with his son around their big backyard. He said:

> It wakes us both up. It's extremely unpleasant for the first few minutes...and then feels great. Our neighbors get a laugh, seeing us out there in our coats and pajamas. But, no more tantrums! He's awake, I'm awake, and we get through the routine on time. I used to be so upset that I could not start work. Now, after that wonderful sound of the bus pulling out—and how I love that sound—I start to work.

In this example, the boy and dad both needed to "kick-start" their morning. Both grumpy, neither handled the morning routine well. By adding exercise, they could complete the rest of the morning. An occupational therapist would probably have described it as a need for sensory input—more stimulation so that they could handle the normal stimulation of the morning.

Learning self-control in daily routines

In our families we teach our children how to organize themselves and maintain self-control. As parents, we teach essential skills such as:

- timing—for example, how long it takes to get ready in the mornings

- balance between time in the home and time at work/school, transitioning between them with items completed in both places

- caring for our physical needs through shopping, cleaning, and body care

- creating space for enjoying family and friends

- caring for others in our society

- spiritual practice.

These bits that have to do with running the home and caring for oneself are called activities of daily living (ADL). Being able to perform them smoothly is an essential part of self-esteem. It is also one of the qualities predicting *resiliency* in life. Resiliency qualities strengthen people to thrive in spite of challenges in life.

As mentioned in the Chapter 1, it is through an attachment relationship that most of us learn how to calm ourselves and reduce stress. We learn to reach out to others for help, starting with our parents. We need to help our children to develop calming and stress reduction by using the normal frustrations of daily jobs and deferred gratification. In the home we also learn how to communicate our thoughts and feelings to others and to listen and care in return. Parents need to practice these communication skills, even when it would be easier simply to separate children who are arguing.

Savvy parents will give children enough responsibility so they are required to use calming, attention-focusing, and flexibility. Parents act as coaches, supporting their children to develop the skills through the demands of homework, chores, and noticing the needs of other family members.

Attachment and caring for others

Attachment includes reciprocity—that is, the noticing of others' needs and not simply our own. People are better at noting the well-being of others when they grow up in a home in which they share tasks and take turns on the priority list. We teach them to be sensitive to the needs of others. For example:

> Jasmine and Jerome had just finished their appointments at the doctor's office. Jasmine, aged eight, had got a sticker from the doctor. Her brother, Jerome, aged nine, had a long history with medical procedures. At the doctor's he had tried to calm himself, failed, and was finally dragged, by his mother and a nurse, from under the exam table for a blood draw. In the aftermath, he did not receive a sticker. On the way home on the train, Jasmine looked at her brother, who was still dripping a few tears and who had vividly failed the doctor's challenge "to set a good example for his little sister." She quietly put her sticker on Jerome's knee. "I'll help you with your cat box job, too," she said. Jerome nodded, wiped his nose on his sleeve, and felt a bit better.

As in the example above, parents' tasks include teaching children to both take and share tasks in an emotionally connected manner. This includes helping everyone in the family. Children also have attachments with their sisters and brothers. Learning how to get along with siblings gives practice in being flexible, waiting, and caring for someone else. Since children are just learning frustration tolerance in their early years, they have ample experience to practice calming themselves when frustrated instead of hitting, yelling, or always having to be first.

Limit-setting, shame, and respect

One goal of limit-setting is to make space for positive activities, as well as to accomplish necessary tasks. The way that we set limits should be respectful of our children and of ourselves. That is, we set limits that are clear, uphold the limits through the use and loss of privileges, and do our limit-setting without acting in a demeaning or frightening manner to our children. *When we frighten our children through excessive shaming or punishment, we reduce the chance that they will approach us with genuine problems.*

Children who can trust their parents are able to use their parents' help into teen years and early adulthood. Wise parents look ahead to the long-term relationship that they want to have with their children. While with a "short, sharp shock" like a smack on the bottom, or a stint of yelling at children, parents may gain immediate, scared obedience, those behaviors reduce parents' effectiveness long term. Children lose respect for their parents and themselves. Children who are wary of their parents tend to lie or sneak. They do not disclose major problems in life.

Parents who smack, swat, and yell should reduce their stress. Good ways to add to parenting skills are reading books (like this one), joining a parenting group, or receiving individual counseling. Parenting books or classes will help parents with ready options when they are frustrated or need to enforce limits. Just having two or three options to choose from will calm parents down.

Parenting can be stressful. Children are likely to model after their parents. When they see parents stressed, and then see stress reduced by their parents' positive self-talk, breathing, putting things into perspective, or taking a break, they are likely to use these methods themselves. Children also respect parents who are emotionally stable. Children who are treated with respect believe in themselves—that they are worthy of respect. They look for relationships in which people respect them. These are long-lasting pay-offs that dwarf a parent's frustrated pay-off from disciplining quickly, carelessly, and thoughtlessly.

Good modeling and positive attitudes shape children's behavior

Most parents think that what they say best describes what they believe. Actually, our actions are more instructive to our children. They demonstrate how we believe that life should be lived. Long before children can understand their parents' words, they are picking up information about the parents' own approaches to life. Our first working model of attachment—whether parents are safe and steady or frightening and unpredictable—is set by seven months of age. Of course, children can change that working model if their parents change, or if they have different parents.

Parents who move smoothly between play and work will provide a great model for their children. Those children will see a model for delaying gratification when needed, but still including pleasure in daily life. If parents have trouble with normal daily limits, their children's reactions will be similar. Parents who spend too many hours watching television or playing with social media will find that their children enjoy the same pursuits—having foreseeable issues with homework and other routines.

Children will notice if their parents complete little jobs daily or weekly, avoiding big pile-ups of problems. Most children will take part in the daily routine. Young children enjoy "helping" their parents with daily tasks: carrying out trash together, loading the dishwasher, sweeping the path, etc. If parents make these tasks positive ones, they help children develop acceptance and even positive feelings about the little jobs that are the "*Keep the Nest Neat*" jobs.

Parents can reinforce positive attitudes towards tasks by showing some satisfaction, accompanied by words such as: "It felt good to get that done! Doesn't the home look good now! We did it together! Thank you for your help." As parents, we want to encourage participation, not in a bedraggled or complaining manner—"I do all of the work around here"—but in a positive way. For example: "It was great that we could work together to make our home look good. You're an important member of the family. I couldn't do this without you."

Helping parents can be the high point of a four-year-old child's day. It sets the tone for the future so that children value being productive. The rub is that including children slows down our daily tasks. But our ultimate goal is not just efficiency with our task lists, but passing on smooth daily routines and positive habits to the next generation.

Parenting roles have changed so dramatically in the last 40 years. Many of today's parents grew up in homes that reflected this societal transition. A grim, overworked determination or a desperate sense of near-chaos may have been your examples as your parents were trying to balance tasks with both parents working full time, or perhaps you had a single parent trying to do it all. Being aware of our pasts, we can "reset" the attitude in our homes.

If the work in the home is simply "too much," then reduce a number of expectations on the list. It is far more important to enjoy daily life than to live feeling fed up except when on vacation. And, it is critical to teach children the rudiments of a positive and smooth daily life. Make a list of your tasks, and then of your priorities. Match them, and then make adjustments.

One parent, who taught in school and had a large family, wrote down all of her tasks, hobbies, and self-care, along with the times required to complete them. She had a 32-hour day. Her husband had lost his previous job, and the new one required him to travel extensively. She was trying to do the household jobs that he could no longer do. Her adjustment included selling two horses that they never had time to ride, and arranging for someone to help with shopping and after-school activities. She funded the help through the sale of their horses. These are the types of adjustments that show a realistic view that we have to live within limits, chosing priorities.

Family jobs—negative versus positive parenting models

Your children may have had negative parenting models before you adopted them or gained custody. Or, you may have been a negative model yourself—complaining, inconsistent, glum, and dissatisfied. It is never too late to make better decisions in how you parent. If you have made a series of poor decisions, then make the next decisions quite good ones, as in the example below.

> Dave, a single parent with three children, got home from work. He entered the house, tired and hungry, having missed lunch due to his child's school-related meeting. He muttered: "No welcome, as usual. No dinner, as usual. Everything's up to me, as usual." Dad proceeded into the kitchen, checked the refrigerator futilely, and then opened the freezer, grabbing a container of ice cream. Before taking his first bite, he opened his mouth wide, broadcasting to his oldest daughter, "Lauren, get down here and clean the kitchen—I need to cook!" Lauren did not appear. He caught sight of the next oldest, Jesse, and said, "Then you get over here since your sister is too lazy to even answer."
>
> Jesse protested: "It's her job. Mine was sweeping the porch and walkway. I did my job. Why me?"
>
> "Because I'm too tired to pull her out of her room," Dad said and sighed. Dad's face changed when his cell phone chimed. He laughed a minute, looking at his cell phone. He quickly texted back. Without eye contact, or without sharing the brief, positive moment, Dad added, "Jesse, get busy."
>
> Jesse found the dishwasher still full of dishes from the evening before. His younger brother, Rama, had not emptied it before breakfast. He shouted, "Daaaaadd, the dishwasher is full." Dad was receding, texting, and eating his dessert before dinner. He did not hear or respond. Jesse considered his options, then carefully stacked all of the dirty dishes in the sink. He began a slow, resentful wipe over the kitchen counter. He made a break for the sidewalk outside. He smiled for the first time since his dad got home.

In this example, the children lacked the parental encouragement or support necessary to teach them to complete an assigned job. Dave showed no pleasure in his family. Obviously, with tasks undone, the children did not rush down to see him. Rather than positively rewarding Jesse with a smile, or inquiry about his day, Dave simply saddled him with another person's job. Dave was modeling pleasure first, tasks second, as he ate ice cream and used his phone. Dave further decreased the positive connection between family members.

This is the second option for Dave:

> Dad is walking in the door, eating an energy bar from his backpack, since he missed lunch. He observes the kitchen morass. He spends a few minutes relaxing, breathing deeply, and stretching.
>
> "Hi Jesse," he says. "Nice job on the walkway. I felt great coming home to that." Jesse smiles and gets close to his dad as he talks about his day.
>
> Dad walks down the hall, locating Rama and Lauren. He calmly walks them into the kitchen together. He says, "We have a problem in the kitchen—let's work together." Supervising the younger Rama, which only involves standing near him, gives Dad time with Jesse and Lauren. They talk about the day and what to have for dinner. After Rama finishes his job, Lauren loads the dishwasher and wipes counters. Dad says, "Thanks, Rama, that is an important job." Dad spends another five minutes with Rama, talking about his day. Everyone gravitates to the kitchen while they talk and Dad cooks. Dad makes an easy omelet, Lauren slices bread, and Jesse makes a salad while Rama sets the table.
>
> They eat a good meal together, which increases connection between family members. At the end of the meal, the family decides on a job change. Rama should unload the dishwasher before bed from now on, so that Lauren can load the breakfast dishes before school. Everyone loads dishes into the dishwasher, straightens the kitchen, and wipes counters. Dad starts the dishwasher. He sets the kitchen timer, telling Rama that when it goes off, Rama will unload the dishwasher. He needs to show Dad that the job is done.
>
> Dad spends a few minutes thinking about his family, and how much he loves them as they finishes dinner. It shows on his face. He feels proud of his parenting. His cell phone is not as interesting. He walks outdoors with Rama and Jesse to enjoy a few minutes kicking the football in the fading light.

What Dave did increased family connection, which was lagging after many hours away from each other. He replaced a minor household challenge with a positive model. He was respectful of himself and others. All the children had access to his attention, which they needed. Last, the children worked on solving a problem together, which helped with family esteem. The older children saw Dave deal with Rama's immaturity by moving his task to a time when he could be supervised. The emphasis was on learning, not shaming. Jesse was praised for doing his job without having had to be reminded.

Routines in children who were neglected

Adoptive parents are often parenting after their children have lived with mentally ill or drug-influenced parents. Their children's early parenting models are poor ones. When in homes of neglect, children do not trust any parents to care for them. Even young children in neglectful homes may use the stove (unsafely), forage in cupboards, scout out the neighborhood, or go for long periods without food during parental lapses. After neglectful parenting it is common for children to both want to take charge of the responsibilities of getting their own food, and resist daily tasks. They have told me that all that tidiness seems unnatural! They want control over food in order to decrease their stress around food scarcity. They want to ignore daily tasks since they do not have much tolerance for frustration.

In another common situation—a start in an orphanage—children are used to having meals and laundry that just appear. Often their daily jobs are few. The daily tasks of running the household seem removed from them. They do not like the introduction of jobs into their lives.

A teen, Olivia, told me: "My mother yells at me because I don't hang up my clothes. But they are in the closet! She should meet me half-way. Before I came here, I only had a half bag of clothes. That was all. Now I have a whole closet full. She wants me to do everything her way. I am trying to please her. I get everything into the closet now and the doors close. But, she isn't satisfied. She has to open the closet, checking it. She should have been Sherlock Holmes, not a mother!"

The combination of Olivia being especially sensitive to shame, and her mother's highly organized manner (the hangers were color-coded), made the issue a high-conflict one. Mom and daughter worked on simple solutions. First, mom removed half of the clothes and forgot about the color-coding. The closet was just too complex. Then, she went through the clothes with her daughter, mentioning how lovely Olivia looked in various outfits. Before bedtime they talked about the next day's weather, choosing two possible outfits for the following day. That way the choices were easy. They put the laundry basket in the bedroom, not the bathroom. The basket did not have a lid, so the dirty clothes actually landed in the basket.

A goal for Olivia and her mother was to make a positive association between organizing and choosing. As Olivia appeared promptly in the morning, and in nice outfits, she received praise and attention. This helped her with positive pairing between organizing and self-esteem.

Positive approaches to routines and organization

Adults are right to be concerned about tasks and routines. Life is complicated in modern society! To be successful, we must have *some* method of organization. Some children/teens will naturally just catch on to these methods. For example, a 17-year-old teen realized that she needed to bring her immunization records to school that day to register for a sports camp. Her parents had already left for work. She hoped that the records would be easily accessible. She reported: "They were in the drawer labeled '*medical records.*' My mom had a folder with my name on it. She had extra copies of my immunization record—probably in case we needed a copy in a hurry." Those easy examples influence teens to copy the template of their parents. They connect ease, relief of anxiety, and organization.

If your home has not included a positive pairing with chores, then "re-setting" your family's automatic approach will be important, and worth the time. Start by noticing your child's accomplishments. For example:

Let me see how you cleaned the living room. Super job! You are an important part of the family. We couldn't keep the home so nice without you. Now we can all relax together in this room. Wait until your mother sees the great job you did.

Stopping to notice the pleasure of a completed task is an important part of changing feelings towards the job.

Similarly, noting the pleasure that is part of a homework project is also helpful in changing patterns of stalling and avoiding the task.

> I was working with a boy who had some learning issues, as well as anxiety over a report. He had a last assignment to complete so that he could pass a high-school class. He did not do it, balking and then failing the class. He was given permission to finish it over the summer.
>
> He brought the report in to me, with his mother in the room. First he wrote the steps to finish the powerpoint presentation. (It was an easy 1-2-3 list.) Then, he began to work on his laptop. He worked steadily. I stopped him. "Are you enjoying the project right now?" I asked.
>
> "Yes. I am. I like it," he replied. I asked him to notice that he enjoyed working on things once he began. I called him two days later, as we agreed, to make certain that he stayed on track.
>
> "I worked the whole way home in the car!" he said. "I even did the bibliography. I finished the class."
>
> I told him how proud I was of him.
>
> A critical piece for this boy was when he noticed that he enjoyed the work once he got going. It followed the feeling of control he got when he laid out the steps to finish his project. His mother read a book, ready to help him if he needed it.
>
> Is it important to notice how he began his work. When he sat down in my office, he handed his mother the project directions. I asked her to hand them back to him. I told him that it was his project, not hers. She was there as a resource, but only if needed. The approach that we used built his confidence, helped him to see the responsibility as his own, and helped him to make an association of enjoying the work.

As parents, we gain enormously when we give positives about the part that our children play in our home. Children need to see themselves as part of the family group, and as positive contributors. Children who have not been in a securely attached relationship in a home may have trouble seeing themselves as a healthy part of the family. They may either take on too much responsibility, wanting to run the family with their rules, or take on too little responsibility, seeing themselves as an island in the middle of the family. They may argue that they have a better, alternative view of family life, or, that the tasks of the family should have nothing to do with them. With these children, having a simple, "then-and-now" discussion can be helpful. Take the following example.

You could say:

> I know that your grandparents liked TV. When you lived with them they allowed you to watch TV or play on the computer all day on Saturday and Sunday, and during the evening the rest of the days. So, you feel that is the way things *should be*. In this family we watch only a little TV. This will be a change for you. We are not trying to be mean. But it would not be fair to you if we allowed you to watch that many hours of TV or play video games. We have learned that your brain would not learn as well as other children's brains. Also, if you spend a lot of time on your computer, it's harder for you to learn how to make friends.
>
> We love you and want to help you through this change. You can come to talk to me about ideas. Sometimes we can compromise. But I do make the final decision because I am responsible for everyone in the family doing well. Our family rule is only one hour of screen time a day. That includes everything electronic.

Parents should spend time doing tasks with children/teens, talking during that time, and enjoying companionship. It will help to pair the connection between the task and positive feelings. And be sure to play a little along the way!

In Appendix C is a list of chores for children, listed in age ranges. I recommend taking a look at the list, thinking of which chores the children could do in your family.

Positive self-talk and positive behavior

Parents will want to help their children with positive "self-talk," that is, the way that we talk to ourselves in order to calm down. *Positive self-talk* sounds like:

- I will try my best.

- I can do it.

- If I need help, I will ask for it. First I will try on my own.

- I will get started.

- I can solve this problem.

- This isn't going to feel so bad tomorrow.

- I've made a mistake, but that only means I'm human.

- I'm really disappointed, but this is not the end of the world.

- My friend has let me down, but I have other friends who have not.

In self-talk:

- We put things into perspective.

- We make plans to solve problems.

- We teach children how to still like themselves or others— even with their imperfections.

Some children have got used to suppressing their feelings. They do not even say that they are stressed or that something bothers them. Notice and inquire about what children are feeling if they bend their fingers back, rub their eyes, wiggle, and pick their nails or lips. Parents can help their child to breathe more slowly, calm down a bit, and then they can gently inquire and talk about what upset their child. As children learn to name the source of the upset, and their feelings about the upset, they learn to get help from us and to calm themselves. This reduces their risk throughout life. They learn to name and face their problems, with support, rather than shutting off their feelings. Over time, this will reduce their risk of turning off their feelings in other ways, like drinking, taking drugs, or cutting themselves.

As parents, we are ideally suited to help our children to talk about their feelings, to use self-talk to put feelings into perspective, and to use physical outlets to reduce too-intense negative moods. When raised with this support, children reach adulthood with healthy, day-to-day habits. Their moods' set-points, or "true North," are balanced and positive.

Chapter 4

Brain-Based Strengths and Deficits, and Developing Executive Functioning

In this chapter, we will look at the way to develop some of the abilities that help children to cope well. There are abilities called "executive functions." These abilities help us to select what we pay attention to, how to keep paying attention, how to shift attention, how to inhibit an impulse, how to put details into a meaningful context, how to notice our impact on others, and how to access our memories, as well as other skills. These abilities, which are brain-based, can be enhanced by parents' efforts. This chapter discusses this process. Parents whose children have some weakness in this area will certainly want to work on these skills. All parents can benefit their children by enhancing the development of executive functions. This chapter is placed prior to the consequences chapter, because careful attention to the skills will result in less need for negative consequences.

Impacts of high stress (cortisol) on children's brains

When children have been exposed to high levels of stress in their formative years, there are impacts on the brain's development. The brain often shows a shape which is characteristic of a high level of stress hormone. The stress hormones prejudice people's brains to be reactive, rather than thoughtful. They shape the brain for high alert versus concentration. When parents are wondering why their child has trouble with a set of behavioral expectations, it is helpful to determine whether or not the child has problems with executive functioning.

Executive functioning defined

People use the term "executive function" because it refers to the Chief Executive Officer (CEO) functions of the brain, or the upper-level command center of the mind.

Executive functioning means that people are able to prioritize, pay attention, switch their attention smoothly, stop themselves from acting on impulse, see the "big picture" (not just the details), motivate themselves, plan and complete projects, remember information easily, and generalize, or apply, learning from one situation to another. The person with strong executive functioning is ideally suited for today's highly organized society. High stress, especially trauma, negatively influences the "executive functions" of the brain. Children under the age of five are particularly at-risk because of the brain's rapid development during early childhood.

The executive function abilities are as follows:

- *Planning.*

- *Organizing.*

- *Classifying.* This means being able to see things in categories.

- *Working memory.* The mind can find information when the person needs to remember the "what, how, when, or why."

- *Emotional control.* The person is able to stop themselves from doing or saying things that occur to them in moments of emotional highs and lows. They try to keep their moods in balance.

- *Inhibiting.* Related to above, people are able to stop themselves from an impulsive act or comment, or to redirect themselves, moving back to what they should be doing.

- *Initiating.* They know when to start tasks. As children get older, they do not need a prompt or push start when something needs to be done.

- *Shifting attention or sustaining attention.* This includes the ability to shift attention from one task to another, or to remain focused.

- *Self-monitoring.* This is the ability to observe yourself mentally, watching your own actions to make certain that you are appropriate for your surroundings.

- *Generalizing.* The person takes information learned in one setting, and applies it in other situations.

Some further descriptions of these are below:

Planning. This ability includes being able to think ahead, or make steps towards a goal. For example, in joining a sports team, planning includes finding out how to sign up, purchasing team clothes, finding out the location of playing fields, and putting the schedule on the calendar with prompts to get there on time.

Organizing time and tasks. Related to the planning above, this ability allows people to see the steps towards reaching goals, and includes understanding and allocating the necessary time to reach a goal. People use these abilities to make progress on school projects, plan for a party, make a shopping list, and prepare dinner.

Classifying or categorizing—organizing space and materials. This relates to the above, but includes being able to understand how to collect and organize meaningfully. The brain must be able to see items in groups or categories, and includes being able to prioritize. For example, items must be sorted so that they are thrown away, filed or put away, or placed in a consistent spot for easy access if they are left out (for example, keys on a hook). Or, all of the warm weather clothes go at one end of the closet, the cold weather clothes at the other.

Working memory. Our working memory is like the chalkboard of the mind. It includes the little things which we make a mental note of for the day. After high stress, the chalkboard is smaller. This is especially true for verbal information. A common conversation is a child saying, "You never told me!" The parent says, "Yes. I did!"

Initiating. When to start? Initiating means that people know when to begin. They prompt themselves, knowing that it is time to start an activity. People with this ability are respected for being self-starters. They generate their own starting bell.

Shifting attention or sustaining attention. This ability refers to the ease with which people are able to move their attention smoothly between tasks or avoid being distracted. It includes continuing to pay attention when it is an effort to do so. A child who cannot turn the television off by himself without a huge tantrum has attention problems.

Self-monitoring. This refers to the ability to measure ourselves against a standard—our own standards for deportment as well as an objective standard. When we are able to hold ourselves to a standard, it is easier to get back on-track if we are drifting. Examples would be the tendency to look at social media on the computer at work, or talking too loudly in a restaurant. A person who is self-monitoring might notice themselves spending "too much" time looking at a personal website during work time, and they will remind themselves to get back to work. Or, when they realize that they are too loud at a restaurant, they will quiet themselves.

Generalizing. This ability allows people to take information from one context and apply it to others. If someone says not to play music loudly because a family member is asleep, generalizing would be knowing to minimize *all* noise, because the family member is asleep.

Executive dysfunction explained

When children have several deficits for their age in the areas above, it is called "executive dysfunction." This is common among some families, simply because of genetics. Since executive functioning continues to develop until the age of 25 years, some people simply develop this later than others. After high stress, many, many children will have executive dysfunction. It makes parenting more taxing. Children with executive dysfunction have many of the following problems:

1. *They have a hard time making a plan.* Parents complain that their children want something to happen, but have no idea how to make it happen or the way it will impact on others in the family.

2. *They do not naturally group or classify items into similar groups.* This makes it hard to put similar items together in order to find them later. The children will struggle to organize a room, a binder, or homework. They will place items in random arrangements, since their brains "see" these items in random arrangements.

3. *They have a hard time with working memory.* As one boy wrote in his journal: "I try so hard at school. I think that I have everything done. But something always seems to go wrong. I miss part of the assignment or forget to turn it in." The working memory includes the short-term memory that allows a person to make a mental list, remembering the items. Or, the person remembers the instructions of a task for the next time the task needs to be done.

   If children cannot see things in categories, as described above, it is much harder for them to remember things. When facts seem unrelated to other information, we do not tend to retain the information.

4. *They will struggle with initiating, or starting a task, or knowing how to approach the task.* Most brains know automatically how to do a task—by breaking down the steps—but these children simply do not seem to know when, where, or how to begin.

5. *They will have a harder time with effortful attention.* It requires effort to sustain attention long enough to have an impact. This effort is necessary in order to make academic progress or to complete most complex tasks.

6. *They are prone to impulses or distractions that take them off-task.* It is harder for them to inhibit impulses that take them off-task. It is hard for them to "tune-out" distractions.

7. *They tend to miss the "big picture."* They see the parts, instead. They may even get stuck on a detail, missing how that piece fits into a larger whole. For example, they might overdo an interesting part of a school project, but miss the other four-fifths of the project. They have also missed the main learning goal that makes the project educational. Or, a child hears that they should not play music loudly because a family member is asleep, but does not deduce that inviting a noisy friend over to play will also be disruptive to the sleeping family member.

8. *They may have processing load issues.* That is, the brain actually gets tired when working hard at remembering, thinking, and learning. It can feel impossible to face more tasks that require brain power, or processing. Most of us can relate to this, remembering long exams or lectures that were draining. Some children feel that fatigue on a daily basis.

9. *They struggle to keep their social lives smooth. Emotional control and self-monitoring skills are weak.* They have problems with emotional extremes. Their relationships tend to be marked by arguments, tiffs, and insults.

All of these issues are common in children who have been adopted from international orphanages or from our foster care systems. Recent research shows that in stable situations, with secure attachments, children's brains show the positive impacts of the home.[1] These children begin to develop more normal stress hormones levels and show improvements in executive functioning. Young people will continue to develop executive functioning into their early adult years.

Low stress and secure attachments seem to provide a window of recovery for the brain. If your child's environment is part of the problem, you can alter the home to best help your child. If the executive functioning seems to be genetic in origin, a low-stress environment is also helpful.

---

1   Fisher, P., Van Ryzin, M., and Gunnar, M. (2011) "Mitigating HA Axis Dysregulation Associated with Placement Changes in Foster Care." *Psychoneuroendocrinology*, 36(4): 531–539.

Effects of executive dysfunction on parent relationships with their children

Parents may feel gloomy after reading the executive dysfunction list, realizing that their children could have a brain-based problem. Parents tend to feel angry or guilty if their children have endured a high-stress early life—depending on whether they think they or someone else caused the problems. Turning anger or guilt into something positive can give parents energy to make changes for their children's futures. An intention of reducing stress for your child is important in order to capture the possibility of a window of recovery for the brain. Lower stress will give the brain the opportunity to develop better executive functioning if the difficulties are stress-related.

It is also important to note again that many families have genetic traits that cause members of the family to have executive functioning problems. Gwen Lewis, a noted neuropsychologist, will ask parents when it seemed that their brains started to "work well," when "life made sense," or when they could "figure things out." One of the parents can usually pinpoint the year. For example, a dad will say, "I was 25 years old." Those responses are both good and bad news. The good news is that the brain development in the early- to mid-20s will greatly benefit the child's executive functioning. The bad news is that the parents will be doing extra careful parenting to assist their child in the interim!

> In one parent discussion, a dad said: "We are not biologically related, but I had many of these same problems as a kid. I was smart, but constantly in trouble over deadlines and impulsive behavior. My home was high-stress. My father and mother argued—a lot. I lived this. I think that I can help my son get his act together. I did. I pulled myself together, got a good job, and have friends. I know that I can help him."
>
> This dad began to help his son with strategies and a positive outlook. He reduced the pressure to "work harder" and began to "work differently." He used many of the suggestions listed on pages 117–127.

It helps us, as parents, when we realize that the issues detailed above are brain-based problems. Your child is not trying to be oppositional or difficult. Parents can teach children to overcome and to compensate. Simply calling children "sloppy," "absent-minded," or "lazy" will further demoralize a child who is already struggling. It is fine to tell children that they may have to work harder than some other children, or that they may need to ask for help, hints, or clues in areas of their school work or chores. Children are not being given an excuse, but an explanation for the difficulties that they face.

Executive dysfunction not only influences tasks; it is the way the brain meets the world.

> A parent, who had three teens with executive dysfunction, summed it up: "I can never assume that things will go smoothly. I need to pay careful attention to friends and school at all times. It is exhausting, but even worse to think of the negative consequences."
>
> The teens did grow up, their brains did develop, and the parents completed their "parenting sentence." When asked later, "Would you like to do it all again?" the parent said: "Are you joking? Of course not! Do you know how many near-misses there were? Getting them all graduated, off to university and jobs, without early marriages or babies—it was nerve-wracking!"

The good news was that these adults all became functioning members of society. But it takes extra functioning by parents, who need to use their brains longer when their teens' brains have not yet developed. Most parents expect to use their brains to help their children, but it can be a surprise to be continuing to do so into the late teens and early 20s.

Prenatal exposure to drugs and alcohol often co-exists with executive dysfunction. There is an interplay of high stress from the parenting environment and genetics (impulsive people are much more likely to use and become addicted to drugs or alcohol).[2] There is permanent brain damage from exposure prenatally to alcohol. But much of the damage that we see in children is due to the stressful, neglectful homes that children live in. In the early years it is hard to know what will be permanent brain damage from prenatal exposure to drugs and alcohol and what will change in a nurturing and learning-rich home.

---

2   Crews, F. and Boettiger, C. (2009) "Impulsivity, Frontal Lobes and Risk for Addiction." *Pharmacology Biochemistry and Behavior*, 93(3): 237–247.

A teen who once was thought to have severe damage from the drugs and alcohol that her birth mother used during pregnancy, was found to be only mildly affected. Vision therapy helped her with visual tracking and reading. Recently she won a state-wide spelling contest. The damage she endured had been largely in the area of executive functioning, which was assumed to be due to prenatal exposure. Once adopted by her relatives at the age of seven years old, she was able to progress in all educational and behavioral areas.

Her mother said: "I once was told that memory and organization would be lifelong problems for her. Now she organizes for us. She functions better than I do in the memory areas!"

While not all children have this wonderful outcome, it is important to provide children with the opportunity to develop to their greatest potential. Parents should not quit when they realize that their child has had "prenatal exposure" to alcohol and drugs. There is a large variation in how much improvement children will show when given appropriate therapies and educational help.

Until recently it was assumed that there was little that people could do to assist executive functioning. However, it turns out that the brain is able to change, growing and developing more capacity in the areas of executive functioning. The next section gives some ways that parents can help.

Helping the development of executive functioning

No matter the origin, children and teens do best if parents start coaching the development of executive skills. The following section has a description of some practical methods. (Please see the resource list for other books and websites.)

1. Help your children to "see" things in categories and to practice planning

For example, lay out the homework in sections. "I have four subjects tonight. I will do them in this order. Then I will read for 20 minutes. Last, I will put all of the homework in my backpack and will tell myself 'great job.'"

Have children tidy the room this way: First, pick up and put away all of the books and papers. Second, sort all of the clothes into clean (to be put away) and dirty (to the laundry). Next, put all of the toys on their shelves. Finally, pull up the comforter on the bed. Stand in your doorway and look at the clean room and smile.

2. Rewards and incentives

Encourage children with mini-rewards as they keep up their good effort. For example, set the timer to begin homework. They will get a reward for beginning on time, as well as for every ten minutes that they sustain attention. The brain is learning to be rewarded by staying on-task, rather than by getting off-task. The mini-rewards can be dimes, two minutes of screen time (TV, hand held games, computer, tablets) or time towards a fun activity. As children progress, parents can space out the rewards. Parents are helping children's brains make the connection between staying on-task and rewards.

One of the reasons that children need frequent rewards is that their brains are not making the long-term connections between staying on-task and a longer-term reward.

Additionally, it is harder for their brain to stay with something if they have a processing-load problem, which means that they have to persist even after their brain gets tired.

3. Initiating

Help children to walk through a task mentally. For example, where would be the place to start on a task, what would you need in the way of materials, and what would the process be like?

If children make a mental map, they can follow that map instead of stopping and then wandering off when they do not know what to do next.

Settle on a beginning time that is exact. In other words, "We will begin at 7:00," which is precise, rather than "after dinner," which is not. Parents can always alter the time saying, "Dinner is running late. We will begin at 7:15 tonight."

If we were working with a person who had trouble initiating, the instruction would best be displayed as:

(a) Where will I start?

(b) What time will I start?

(c) Visualize the task.

(d) Break the task into small steps—list them.

(e) What materials will I need for each step?

(f) Set goals. What is today's goal for the task?

(g) How do I appear to others right now and while I work?

Parents can model the steps above as they work on tasks, talking through their own process. They can write lists and share them with their children.

When I have children who are in need of help with executive functioning, I like to use the time in my office to model this. I organize the time in therapy into a list of what we will work on and the order in which we will work. The children and I co-create the lists. We decide which materials in the office to use. It helps children to stay on-track during the time together, but also gives them freedom to bring in their own thoughts, feelings, and creativity. A side benefit is that children are not so controlling when there is a structure for our time together.

4. Making plans and putting organization to work

It seems to work best to plan "just enough" with children. Too much detail makes it hard to see the priorities. (It is also dull.) Too little and there is chaos.

You might approach a situation by saying, "Let's make a plan so that everything goes well—this should be a fun activity to plan!" I like to frame the planning time as enjoyable. It can be part of the anticipation. We start with the goal, or objective. An example below is of a parent, Jill, planning with her child, Thomas, in a manner that builds executive functioning.

> "Tuesday is a half-day at school. Let's do something fun for the afternoon! What could we do to have a good time, getting home before dinner? Grandma and Grandpa are coming for dinner that night."

Thomas responds: "Let's go to the video arcade! Or, maybe we could go to the zoo to see the new elephant! I'd like to take a friend."

Jill might respond, "What are some of the important thing for us to consider?"

Thomas says: "Maybe whether my friend would like the zoo or the arcade best. Or, maybe I should check the weather report."

Mom praises Thomas's thinking ahead by saying, "Great thinking ahead! Wow!"

Notice that Jill is being vivid and positive in noticing Thomas's planning. This "noticing" helps to encourage the development of planning.

Jill and Thomas discuss which child would enjoy either the zoo or the arcade. Then, they discuss how to run on time for the grandparents. Jill gives facts on distance and time-frames for a friend who lives closer to or further from the zoo or arcade. She also helps Thomas think through what would happen if the friend's parents were late collecting their child.

Thomas makes a plan with steps: Check the weather report. Choose either the arcade or the zoo. Invite a friend who would enjoy the activity. Arrange to pick up the friend after school. Decide what time to leave the zoo or arcade. Ask if the friend's parents are able to pick up the friend at Thomas's home at the end of the activity—if not, leave the activity 15 minutes earlier.

While the process above is labor-intensive, it gives Thomas a template that he can use again and again as he develops executive skills. The next time that there is a similar event, Mom can say: "Remember the planning for the zoo? This is almost the same." Then, Jill asks Thomas if he can see how it is different and similar.

This type of organization can be used for relationship issues as well as tasks. Within my office, when we are working on a decision, we may use a list of pros and cons. The list will include children's thoughts and feelings—as well as the consequences. Or, children will make a plan to calm, to make amends, or to approach a difficult situation.

After working with me for a series of sessions, children often start to copy those templates, picking up the markers, dividing the paper, and making plans. These are simple models that help them to organize information, to calm themselves, and to plan. The process helps their executive functioning develop as they stick to the plan. Examples of plans for use at home are included in Appendix D.

5. Explain the big picture and how a particular item fits into the big picture

For example, I explained to a girl how learning her math facts would help her to be a veterinarian. She and I role-played needing to determine the correct medication for the weights of a big dog or a small dog. She decided that math facts were a relevant part of her education.

Children with executive dysfunction simply do not see all of the connections between details and a larger picture. That seems to be a reason for so much of their confusion and their lack of compliance. Parents who introduce information by putting it into a context will have much higher compliance. Over time their children may come to say: "Is there some meaning that I am not getting? What is the purpose of this?" They begin to use their experiences to build better executive functioning.

An 11-year-old boy got into the car after a summer camp. "You were right, Mom," he said. "All of your hard work on manners worked. I just got 'Camper of the Week.' The counselors said that I knew how to listen and show respect. I answered when they spoke. You said that people would appreciate it, and you were right."

The parent in this example posed the skill-set as being long term in his best interests in forming relationships. This tween boy saw it as something that mattered in the "big picture." Even though he had some executive dysfunction, he was guided to understand the larger context. He had higher functioning than most peers without these issues.

6. Recognize the realities of processing loads

"Processing load" refers to how much people are able to think about, with focus, before their brains are too full to absorb more. Physical education classes can be arranged to give children breaks in their school schedules. Some parents are careful screeners of school, making certain that necessary subjects are taught when children are still fresh. They look at using the limited "real estate" of their children's brain in the best possible manner.

If your child has processing-load issues, you may arrange for some recovery time before homework. If children are simply too brain-weary to begin homework, it makes sense to let them play for a while.

Some things seem to drain brains. Handheld games, or video gaming systems, can be especially problematic for children with executive dysfunction that co-exists with prenatal exposure or with attention problems. The children may explode when asked to transition into activities that require focused attention.

Always use video games as rewards for children *after* they accomplish activities that require focus. And do limit them, even after chores are done. It is not really an issue of the screens themselves, but more of a concern that children are missing out on making friends. Video and computer games stimulate the centers of our brains that are reward centers for social engagement. The problem is, our children have a sense of social reward, without any real social connection. They are not making friends or learning about each other.

7. Self-monitoring and noticing the feelings of others

Most of us have a mental model about the people around us—their feelings, thoughts, and motivations. We watch how others affect us and vice versa. In other words, we have a "theory of mind." That is, we understand the mind of another and our own. Even if we are slightly "off," it gives us a broad brush way of predicting and interpreting the actions of others—without losing sight of our own interests or feelings. *This is the core of emotional intelligence.*

We can encourage the development of emotional intelligence by encouraging our children to develop knowledge about ourselves and others. This is not done intrusively, but with warmth and curiosity. For example: "Madelyn is frowning and her head is down. What do you think might have happened to make her feel like that?"

Parents can help children learn the art of recognizing helpers or potential problems before events. For example: "Disneyland has a 'lost children' location. It is here on the map. Why do you think that they came up with that location? How long would you be gone before I would get scared? If you need to find the place on the map, how would you go about it?"

It is also helpful to ask leading questions that will help children learn to predict social outcomes. For example:"Should you ask your best friend what she thinks about the time and the day before you set the time for your party? What do you think she would think about you, if you chose a date, being especially careful that she could come?"

Parents can help their children to learn about what others are thinking, basically encouraging healthy "mind-reading." I strongly suggest this approach when with children, commenting on various choices and anticipating the respective feelings of others as a result of the choices. These discussions, over time, can have interesting results.

> Mateo's parents had worked hard developing his self-monitoring. They knew that they had success when they overheard him talking to his friend. The food-oriented, rapidly growing 13-year-old Mateo was at his friend's home for dinner. He complimented his friend's mother on her recipe, cleared his dishes, and helped with the clean-up afterwards.
>
> He said to his friend: "Mothers love this. They cook extra for you if you do this. Tell her that you appreciate her. Tell her something about the cooking—like, 'I appreciated the balance of the lemon and spices in the main dish.' You should always be nice to the cook!"
>
> Mateo's social intelligence improved the performance of the cooks in his life as well as his popularity!

Parents who are working with children/teens on self-monitoring do best with a playful, curious approach. I suggest helping children with thinking and observing "in the moment." That "real time" approach helps our children to find the learning in similar situations. Their brains are collecting relevant information when they are actively engaged in the process. If we teach in a dry way, or lecture in situations that are outside of "real time," it is harder for children's brains to find and apply the information in the future.

8. Managing emotions

Parents are in the best position to teach children how to calm, or how to think about emotional situations. Keeping young children close, while you hold your own emotions in check, will give you the chance to help your child. Your older children will learn that you are a support when they are upset. The patterns that they develop in your home will be used throughout the rest of their lives. This process was described in Chapter 3, so is only mentioned here.

9. Helping working memory

Parents may want to teach their children to use lists or prompts in order to help their memories. I like to show children my lists, with items checked off as I complete them. It helps children to see that everyone needs a bit of help in the memory department. When children are off-task, I do not want to shame them unduly for not remembering, but I do ask them questions like:

- What are you to be doing right now?

- What are you to do next?

- Do you need a hint, or can you find the information in your head?

- Take a minute to think.

- Great job thinking. You remembered!

When children have memory issues, they can begin to rely on parents for every prompt. This is exhausting for parents and worries them. Parents wonder if they will have to follow their children around for the rest of their lives! I like to ask children to try to remember. Then, if they cannot, I ask them if they want a hint or a clue. It might take children longer to find the information, but our goal is to have them stretch and use their memories. For children who are trying to remember, parents can provide a friendly hint given with a positive, light touch. Try to give a hint instead of the entire answer.

I recommend that parents make a big deal when children do remember. Most children from high-stress backgrounds have brains that have been shaped to remember what is vivid or emotional. Making praise vivid and emotionally rewarding helps all of us to remember and repeat a positive event.

10. Short-term and longer-term memory, and chunking information

Short-term memory comes in short segments, called "chunks." These are specific details such as a number, a person's name, or a task on a "to-do" list. Most children can retain two to three chunks for about 15–20 seconds in their normal working memory. For example, a three-chunk request might be: "John, please pick up your track shoes. Put them in your gym bag." These chunks (bits to remember) help us to store information long enough to complete tasks successfully. John has three chunks in the example. He needs to locate the trackshoes, pick them up and then put them into the gym bag. Over time, he will needs to move that short-term grouping into longer-term memory. On days that he runs, he always places his track shoes in his gym bag.

Both short and long-term memory improve if the information is novel, interesting, or meaningful. In the example above, parents can increase the interest or meaning to John by saying: "John, you got right on that! Great! Come get a high-five. You will have everything you need for the race today. Do you want to get a treat for after the race?

In order to move short-term memory information into a long-term memory, we can include a hands-on application right after the chunking.

For example, "John, the name of your new track coach is Ms. Jones. Would you please write her name down on my phone contact list? Just think, Ms. Jones on our phones. It rhymes."

John laughs and adds, "Ms. Jones, on our phones, runs my bones."

Our working memory can be strengthened. When building memory, it helps to break down new information into small steps. For example, the new information on executive functioning in this chapter has been described, listed in a bulleted list, and numbered and described in terms of deficits. The options for helping executive functioning were subheaded and numbered yet again. By the time you finished the section, you probably had the information mentally organized.

Another way to help working memory is to associate it with previous learning from similar learning experiences. In John's example, above, parents could mention that track is like football was. The sport bag always has special sports equipment: shoes, a uniform, water, etc. We have a coach whose name we memorize. When we want to find out where we will be playing or running, we ask by giving the name of our coach or school. We get to the playing fields a little early, since we often have to walk out to the right fields. Children enjoy knowing what will happen next. These comparisons help them to identify which things will be similar. They like the predictability and mastery of knowing how things work.

All of us enjoy the chance for a "hands-on" approach when trying to remember something. In John's example, he was able to use his hands to enter in the name of the coach. It helps memory to let children use their hands or bodies to show you what they know.

Little songs, rhymes, acronyms, or plays on words are also helpful in improving memory. These can be introduced as games. They make learning routines fun. Parents are not so likely to be tuned out if they use these playful approaches.

11. Focusing attention on purpose—effortful attention

When children have a hard time focusing attention, it helps to use the part of the brain that is best at handling multiple streams of information. The best area for this is almost always our visual area.[3] So, we will want to use visual more than verbal reminders or prompts. I like to get close to children when trying to gain their attention. If you are calm, your calm signals will help them either stay on-task or move their attention to where it should be. Just by having you sit close by, many children are able to stay on-task, focusing for longer. Their parent is a calming reminder. In addition,

---

3   Siegel, D. (2013) "Working with Attachment and Temperament in the Development of Adult Personality." Training in Seattle, WA.

children are less prone to attempt a short-cut, taking off before a task is done.

A visual prompt sheet for the day will help children to stay on-task. This can be a written or visual schedule. I like to put rewards on the list. That way, children are rewarded for focusing their attention, not for getting off-track. An after-school list for a nine-year-old might look like this:

> 3:00 Home from school. Put away coat and shoes, eat a snack, get hugs, talk a little.
>
> 3:30–3:45 Homework laid out and items gathered to do homework.
>
> 3:45–4:00 Work hard on homework.
>
> 4:00–4:10 Little break to play with dog.
>
> 4:10–4:30 Work on homework again. Homework done. Homework put in backpack. Yippee!
>
> 4:30–5:30 Free time.

Children like to know what they should be working on during certain time-frames. Younger children do well with visual schedules that have simple pictures rather than words. Typically, the schedules include about five to ten items, morning or night, depending on the age of the child.

If children have learned that they have lots of options through their lack of focus, it can be difficult to work with this oppositional habit. A preventative approach is best! If children have already formed oppositional habits, I like to involve them in the big picture talk on how much easier life will be if the task is not hanging over their head. Or, how nice it would be to feel approved of, rather than disapproved of.

Most children are in favor of a task being "over with" in a short time-frame. They are often amazed that the task is so short once they focus and work hard. If you are a parent attempting to break the child's habit of wandering off, then I suggest that you stay next to your child while you set a new habit of following through. It ultimately will take less time than your tracking of a fast, stealthy child over the span of hours.

Sometimes the reason children cannot pay attention is because they are anxious. It is much harder for any of us to use our memories or focus when we are stressed. I encourage some deep breathing, especially emphasizing the breathing out, to help with anxiety. Or, have children run on the spot (run in place) or do jumping jacks for two minutes. (Take the opportunity to join them. It will help both of you to think and feel better.)

I like to ask children if there is something that they are worried about. After talking about the problem that bothers them, children are often able to relax and focus better.

Additional help in assisting executive functioning

There are some helpful organizational applications that can be loaded onto phones or tablets. Children like to use the apps in order to check off their tasks. This is a constructive way to use technology. I have older children loading their homework and schedule onto the computer. As long as the children do not get "lost" in the technology, it can be fun to use the tools on the phone or tablet. Please see the suggestions in the Resource List at the end of the book.

You may be looking at the lists in this chapter and reflect that you, or definitely people you know, seem to have executive dysfunction. (Many couples decide that their partner has a significant brain-based problem after about a year of marriage.) Adults with executive dysfunction often partner with a person who is endowed with strong executive functioning. This is a wise choice. The parent with stronger executive functioning is the best choice for follow-though on tasks, homework, and schedules.

> Shannon, who was a stay-at-home parent, told me that she had always struggled with time, organization, and distractions. Her own mother used to become silent and grim as Shannon's childhood failures came to light. "Well, I don't refuse to speak for the rest of the day like my mother did when she was angry," she said. "Instead, I yell at the kids about their missing assignments. Then they get angry...and I cry."

She and her husband shifted parenting tasks so that homework help moved to the dad, Paul. Paul was an organized man, who used visual prompts himself. Soon the kids' homework tracking was hooked into the family computer, with alerts and daily lists. Homework time was restricted to a 40-minute slot in the evening. Paul had more work to do at home, but was willing to do it. He enjoyed the peace that it brought to the household. Paul did have a tendency to over-organize, though. Shannon's strengths showed up as she insisted on positive mealtimes (without Paul's commentary on how many grams of protein and fiber each child ate) and free, imaginative play time for the children.

Children with executive dysfunction are at-risk for having school failures, even when they have normal intelligence. Part of being a capable parent for these children is helping to attend to their need to organize. Parents who are active in supporting their children's educational attainment are safeguarding their child's future and self-esteem. We do not want children to give up on themselves and their schooling.

You may recognize yourself, from reading the above, as the caring parent of a child with problems in executive functioning. However, you can develop a supportive approach with your child around schooling. I suggest that you do not label, but do let your child know that they learn differently. Essentially, you have a conversation that includes the facts that: 1) Your child's brain sometimes skips some things; 2) Your child is smart enough to achieve; 3) Your child may need to have some extra help to get the big picture or to start and to complete tasks.

A sample conversation, with information pitched kindly and honestly, sounds like this:

"Your school teaches in one way." (At this point I like to draw ten kids' heads on a piece of paper.)" If you take ten kids, six will learn that way best." (Circle six heads.) "One of the ten kids will learn more slowly." (Circle another head.) "The other three kids will learn just as quickly, but have to be taught a little differently. You're one of the three kids. You're just as smart. But, you'll miss some of what they are talking about at school. Tell the teacher the part that you understand, and the part that you don't. Also, ask us at home. That way you'll understand the main idea, or get why the teacher is doing something that does not make sense to you."

Children may respond by saying, "Am I messed up?"

"No," parents answer. "Your brain's a detail brain. And, your brain also likes to look around for interesting things. If we were people from earlier times, you would be the one to be the look-out for danger. But, since we send everyone to school to learn the same way, no matter which way their brain works best, we'll just have to make the best of it. There are lots of jobs for people who notice interesting things or whether details are right. Also, your brain will probably keep growing until you're 25 years old. The 'big picture' and organizing yourself will keep developing."

"You'll have to work a little harder than some kids. So, you'll just learn to be a bit more of a hard worker. If you miss assignments, or don't get the main idea, just tell us. We won't be mad at you. We'll work on this together. You can still have a good future and a good job someday."

Some kids will find this to be too much information to handle all at once. Parents can modify by giving the information in bites, or in a simplified version. The sample is simply a template, showing what could be said to a child with issues of attention and organization, who tends to miss the "big picture." The parent in this example is lending support, sensitivity, and optimism.

In actual fact, the conversation really did take place (though with slightly different wording). This child became an adult who finished a university degree and now currently handles complex accounting issues. His executive functioning *did* continue to develop into adulthood. His detail orientation is used to advantage in his profession. He uses computer-based technology to help him with organization. He continues to have close relationships with his family.

Homes of children with executive dysfunction should have few distractions

If parents want children to walk through a room, not getting distracted, then the distractions are best put away, out of sight. When children already have problems seeing things in categories, a house with order and categories becomes important. Messiness makes it much harder for children to find things and to focus—whether or not they are the ones to cause the mess. The problems with organization are made worse in a distracting or messy setting.

When children have trouble with distraction, it helps to have key phrases to get them back on-track. One mentioned earlier is: "What should you be doing right now?" Children should repeat back the task or activity that is supposed to be their focus.

Certain things are known distractions/sinkholes (e.g. having computer games, handheld games, or television readily available). There is now some evidence that these activities not only are more tempting to children with attention deficit disorder (ADD), but worsen their attention problems.[4] Discuss kindly with children the "why" of these items as distractions. One parent, who was prey to a pre-holiday commercial advertisement, bought an X-Box system, with games, for her two boys, both of whom had diagnosed executive dysfunction and ADD. With great woe, the system was locked into the trunk of their mom's car within a month. "They are addicts!" Mom said. "Nothing was getting done. They fought and wept when the system was turned off for the evening. My younger boy was wailing, "You stole my gift from Santa."

I strongly suggest that parents of distractible children rent video systems for short-term rewards, rather than buying them. If you must buy them, then I suggest that you, the parents, own the system. That way you can kindly give time to your child as a reward. It is quite difficult to explain to children with executive dysfunction how the system is theirs, but that you are in control.

Attention deficit disorder

While this section is written for parents whose children have attention problems, most parents can benefit from the suggestions. Effortful attention is part of executive functioning, but many children with ADD do not have executive dysfunction. And, children with executive dysfunction may have few problems with attention but more difficulties with other aspects.

4   Gentile, D., Swing, E., Khoo, A., and Lim, C.G. (2012) "Video Game Playing, Attention Problems, and Impulsiveness: Evidence of Bidirectional Causality." *Psychology of Popular Media Culture*, 1(1): 62–70.

The rate of children who have ADD is high among children who have been prenatally exposed to drugs, alcohol, or toxins. It is also higher among children who were adopted. Of course, some of those children had prenatal exposure to drugs, alcohol, or other toxins. Moving preschool children between families increases the rate of problems.[5] When children have problems with sustaining or shifting attention, we can give them additional assistance by organizing the home in particular ways. As mentioned in the previous section, we do best using visual information. The visual processing center of our brain, our visual cortex, is good at managing multiple streams of information. Our auditory systems (speaking and listening) are best used without other stimulation. Parents can try the following:

- Reduce background noise.

- Use visual reminders more than verbal ones.

- Compose weekly flow sheets that display family events, information, and obligations. These should be simple summaries, not cluttered. (Whiteboards are used effectively in hospital. Try using these in your home.)

- Have "prompts" on children's or teens' computers, so that they get a notice about important assignments or appointments.

Help for attention problems at home: making attention a priority at home

I suggest that parents create a home that promotes focusing attention. If a project is out on a work space, then have just one project at a time on that work space. Try not to not have distractions when children are trying to focus. For example, do not talk on the telephone next to someone who is trying to complete a school homework project.

Your proximity is helpful to children who are having a hard time completing projects. Your presence can be a calm reminder to stay on-track. When the person has an impulse to drift off to

---

5   Fisher, P., Kim, H., and Pears, K. (2009) "Effects of Multidimensional Treatment Foster Care for Preschoolers (MTFC-P) on reducing permanent placement failures among children with placement instability." *Child Youth Services Review*, 32: 541–546.

more interesting turf, you are a physical reminder to stick with the activity. When your child begins to look around, it is a great time to mention that they are doing a good job of sticking with the task, even when it is difficult. Sometimes parents give a choice to children. For example: "Do you think that you would like a break for five minutes, or just finish? I think that you are about ten minutes away from being done." It helps children to own their own choices, being part of the process.

Parents have a balancing act. They will want to calm overall anxiety, but sometimes boost children's minor stress. A minor spike in stress causes us to speed up, expend energy, and try hard. But daily, unrelenting high stress saps our joy and disrupts attention. One such example is Emma, aged nine years old.

> Emma was afraid that she would be "held back," if she scored low on her standardized tests. Emma was frightened and anxious, although the test was a month away. Her mother and I reassured her, telling her that children were not "held back" in her school because of test results. But I did boost Emma's "adaptive stress," that is, the increase of stress that helps people to meet a challenge. I pointed out that she needed to complete her homework within the next hour in order to go to the book fair at school that evening. The first stressor was debilitating. The second stressor helped Emma to push herself to meet a goal. (Emma enjoyed the book fair.)

Some children do not make connections between what they are asked to do and the consequences of doing that task—or not. Parents will often need to make cause and effect connections for children that might seem obvious. For example:

> Emma's mother told her to hurry with her homework so that she could go to the book fair. That was not concrete enough for Emma. Instead, she was motivated by the specific timeline. Over time, Emma learned to compose an evening schedule with a timeline. She looked at the whiteboard, writing a schedule for herself that included family events. Because she was a bright girl with a busy single parent, she began writing a schedule for her sister, as well.

Schedules like these help children to develop a sense of time. The use of a strategy helps children to feel more in control. It reduces high stress, but increases the adaptive stress to "get moving."

Children usually like to order their choices by writing them down. Younger children are able to use picture sequences. For younger children the choices are simplified. Returning to the example earlier in the chapter of the child planning to go to the zoo before the grandparents came for dinner, parents could propose the choices as either the zoo or indoor gym (more appropriate for younger children than the arcade). The pictures could be the weather (picture of sun or rain), phone (picture of phone for the call to a friend), the time to leave the activity (picture of clock on 5:00) and home (picture of grandparents' faces). The pictures could run from top to bottom on a page. Numbers could be written beside each picture.

These plans reduce chaos and tantrums. Children learn to think more reasonably. I like to have prompts or aides to help children, as well as the plans. These might be a sand timer (hourglass), egg timer, or visual timer. (The visual timer is listed in the Resource Section.) All of these show the progression of time, which can be a hard concept for children.

Other ways that help children to organize are keeping a calendar, organizing phone and address books, keeping logs of phone calls in and returned, handling money with a saving system, and helping to plan family social events. Children with ADD should be encouraged to use computers or tablets to help them with organization. A computer prompt is neutral. Parents are saved the dreary task of prompting so often.

As children get older, you may want to show them your organizational system. If you do not have one, this is a great time for you to start one. You will need a simple system that children are able to copy. You can show your system to your kids, saying: "These are my files. The medical files have green labels. Money records are in blue. Let's look at some ways to organize when we go to the store. Which do you like?"

I like to use stacking plastic drawers for family items that everyone needs. There is a drawer for passports and birth certificates, one for immunizations and current medical information, one for spare keys, one for pet records, one for major and current receipts, and one for tickets. Asking children and teens to put things into the drawers will help them to get used to a system.

Summary on executive function and dysfunction

All parents will be working on the areas of executive function. The reason that this section is presented prior to the discipline section is that executive dysfunction is not a discipline issue. It is brain-based and will need some extra special effort from you, as the parent. If your children are showing weaknesses in executive functioning, you will be parenting in a more mindful, deliberate fashion. As you lend your children support and compassion, you will continue the development of your attachment. Children who are not getting support with executive dysfunction tend to have stress on their attachments. They feel increasingly alone, guilty, and distant. As mentioned earlier in the chapter, researchers are showing the ability of adoptive parents to help with the development of executive functioning through the development of secure attachments and stable homes.

Some parents' favorite resources on executive functioning are listed in the Resource List at the end of the book. Many of these were developed for children with a diagnosis of autism. They also work beautifully for other children who need extra help with executive functioning.

Chapter 5

Carrots and Sticks, Rewards and Limits

Most parents prefer the smiles and rewards approach when shaping children's behavior. It would be wonderful if we could raise our children with only positive "noticing" of their successes. If they made a poor choice, we might offer a sage reflection of what they should have done—followed by some sort of restitution that our children quickly volunteered to do. Sadly, the human condition is such that there comes a time when a negative consequence needs to occur. With some children, that time seems to come often. In this section we will discuss the use of rewards and negative consequences (discipline) through which we shape the behavior of our children.

If parents have temperamentally easy children, they may find that they almost never have to use the negative end of consequences.

> A parent, who had been an easy child, said: "My parents had me sit on my bed to think about things when I misbehaved. That was all that it took to have me change my behavior."
>
> Her daughter, who had been prenatally exposed to alcohol before birth, responded to the "sit on the bed" consequence by pounding on the door and wailing for over an hour. This parent needed more than the basic parenting tools in her parenting toolbox! (The door could have used the toolbox, as well.)

Most children will need some negative consequences along the way, but you can strive for more of a positive to negative ratio at all times. I like to think in terms of a 7:1 ratio. That is, positive glances, verbal reassurances, nice gestures and touches, and "noticing" are all positives that occur about seven times to every one time that you are correcting your children.

Noticing behaviors

A powerful positive way to shape behavior is by "noticing" your child's positives. Do notice when children share, load stuff into the car without stepping on each other, help out, show kindness, offer to help, come promptly to dinner, and do chores without reminders. A parent might say, "They should do that without having to be thanked!" But, this is exactly the pattern that noticing will cement. Our goal is to make positive patterns. Children remember best the actions that are noticed and commented on by others. It helps keep them on a path of positive interaction, getting attention in a positive manner.

Types and amounts of rewards

The more children need to *create* positive patterns, the more we will have to use rewards. Rewards can be given in the form of stickers, gum (sugarless is recommended), minutes of TV or video time, nickels or dimes, or time doing something fun with parents or friends. With younger children, or children with short attention spans, it helps to use a positive reward many times per day. I like to have about 20–30 rewards for children daily when we are trying to establish positive routines. That is why the rewards are in small amounts.

> The mother of a 13-year-old was tired. She complained to me: "My daughter is just nasty. I don't even like her. Everything is a battle. I love her, but wonder why I do. She's just not fun to be around."
>
> I suggested that she begin using a reward system of dimes. She began noticing and reinforcing positives at least 20 times a day. She called me saying: "I thought that you were nuts when you suggested this, but it's working. Now I know the secret of this. I like myself better when I'm noticing all of the positives. The tension between us is way down. My daughter is smiling at me. When she bought me a chocolate bar with the dimes, I thanked her. Then, I went into my bedroom and just cried. I realized that we had got to the point where neither of us could do anything right. We're doing so much better now. She still has problems and needs limits, but we like each other again. She's trying to please me."

When children are hesitating before a nasty word or action, do comment on their impulse control in a positive manner. For example, if a child stops to think before speaking, comment on that. For example: "Good thinking, Jenny. You think before you speak."

> Perhaps Billy picks up a play train to throw at his brother, Sam. His action is a knee-jerk reaction after Sam tripped over the train set-up that Billy and his sister had been working on for an hour.
>
> As Billy hesitates before throwing, you could say: "Wow. You were angry, thought about throwing, and didn't. Wonderful."
>
> Billy replies, "I thought about how much I didn't want to have to do Sam's chores as a consequence!"
>
> "Great thinking," Dad says. "You can fix your track in about ten minutes. The chore would have added another 20 minutes."
>
> Sam says: "Sorry, Billy. I didn't mean to trip on your set-up. I'm sorry that it's messed up."
>
> Billy replies: 'I was just mad for a minute. I can do it again. It's OK."

In the example above, the parent's "noticing" and positive action changed the whole emotional tone of the scene. This is much more effective than a parent saying, "How dare you raise your hand towards your brother!" The point was that Billy stopped himself, however momentarily. The parent's job is to stretch the hesitation into longer-term self-control.

The younger the child, or the more help that they need in moving to a new pattern, the more often we reward them. For example:

> Kenyetta, aged six, was in a custody arrangement, living with her father one week, her mother the next, each with a different day-care arrangement. Kenyetta was confused and looked annoyed for about half the time. She was not picking up beginning to read and acted as if her teacher's instructions could be ignored.
>
> The parents wanted to work things out so that Kenyetta would thrive. They realized that they had evenly split Kenyetta's time, but the schedule interfered with attachment and development.
>
> They agreed that Kenyetta should be at her mother's home every week, with an after-school, in-home nanny (a college

student who needed a part-time job and who was willing to use the reward system). The decision was based on the mother's work schedule, whose teaching timetable matched the school schedule best. Dad would take Kenyetta every Friday night through to Sunday morning every other week.

Both parents began to reward Kenyetta with stickers, minutes of a video, or a nice touch (pat, hug, shoulder squeeze) for:

- listening when they talked—with eyes towards the parent or nanny

- answering people who spoke to her

- hesitating when asked to "stop," and later, "stopping" when asked to "stop"

- picking up after herself

- cooperating with hair care, teeth brushing, bedtime routine, coming to meals, etc.

The rewards came many times per day. She could save her rewards for a bigger one. But initially she was simply not able to think past a half-day.

When Kenyetta did not cooperate, the parents waited her out. They did not allow her to turn on the television or to play until she cooperated. Sometimes they held her hands while they picked up her toys together. "I would rather do it myself!" She would yell.

"Wonderful," her parents said. "We think that you can pick up your own toys." Then, they would reward her when she picked up, ignoring the "huff."

Over the next few months, Kenyetta developed a basic compliance habit and settled down to learn in school. As she improved, the parents phased out the number of sticker and video minute rewards for the first target behaviors (answering, picking up after herself, eye contact), but moved to rewarding new behaviors:

- smoothing the comforter on her bed, putting clothes in the laundry, and sweeping the floor (basic chores)

- calming herself down with deep breathing or "giving herself a hug" (putting her arms around herself and squeezing)

- saying "sorry" when she said mean things

- speaking to parents and others with respect.

In Kenyetta's case, her initial custody arrangement was disrupting her basic attachment and body rhythms. She was not learning compliance or calming. Both parents worked for her best interests. They gave her a steadier residential schedule. Then, they used a reward system that was consistent and frequent, spacing out rewards as gains were cemented.

This example shows the necessary pairing between parents working on what is stressing their child, and a reward system that encourages new behaviors.

Limits and enforcing limits with negative consequences

Everyone needs to learn to live within limits. As mentioned earlier, a difficult, but necessary part of parenting is enforcing limits.

No matter how fun or enticing we make compliance, parents need to hold the line. The battle metaphor is intentional. Some children make it seem so easy—for example, the mother who described sitting on her bed as an effective deterrent. Other children have had life experiences or temperaments that make control a battle line.

As mentioned in Chapter 3, after we work on teaching children to calm, then we work on compliance patterns with rewards. But negative consequences do need to be included in the arsenal. When we use negatives, it seems to work best when we keep a positive reward (compliments, pats, physical rewards) to negative reinforcement in a 7:1 ratio. We want our children to learn to get our attention in a positive manner.

Parents cannot succeed in working on many aspects of children's behavior at a time. Instead, picking one or two target behaviors over a two-week period seems to be best. New behavior patterns take effort. Sometimes, as parents, we start correcting everything that passes our radar. This is simply too much correction for most children. I like to put seven "coins" in my pocket. Once I have "spent" seven, I will make a correction. Of course, this means that I have to be working with a strong, positive margin.

If you are a parent unable to keep to this ratio, then consider whether your child could be too stressed to be developing positive behaviors, as in the case of Kenyetta above. Perhaps your child needs an assessment to determine what is blocking development. Sometimes trauma, grief, medical conditions, or attention deficit disorder (ADD) and other learning issues are making our children's lives complicated. And, as discussed in Chapter 4, children with executive dysfunction need a lot more help in how their homes and school lives are arranged by their parents. With more information, parents are able to make a plan that includes necessary home strategies, learning help, and/or psychological help for their children or for their family.

Dealing with small bean counters—making up time with jobs or lost pleasures

When we set a limit, we have to be willing to back that limit up. When setting up a limit, I like mentally to add what I will counter with if a child does not comply. This becomes a mental habit. In this section, we will look at some options.

> Liliana, aged nine, and her brother, Edwin, aged seven, were not motivated to go to school on time. They liked being at home. Their single mother, worried for her job, was frantic to drop them at school so that she could get to work on time. After ample prompts, evening preparation for a smooth morning, and discussion, it was time to use negative consequences.
>
> Liliana's mother enforced having the children go to bed twice as many minutes early as the minutes that they were late to school. At school, the teacher had Liliana miss recess for as many minutes as she was late to school. (While missing recess was not Mom's first choice, she did not interfere.) The children's self-interests were impacted. After two weeks of complaining and tantrums about the limits, both children began to comply. The previous school year, the children were late over half of the time. The lateness to school rate improved to once a month.
>
> Liliana and Edwin were bean counters. They were able to block out their mother's entreaties to "please, please, get in the car!" As miniature accountants, they realized that they had more free time at home by running late. When the equation changed so that their free time was reduced, they changed their behavior.

Some children are quite calculating about costs and benefits. If you are a parent who is parenting such a child, the equations will have to work in your favor. Your child may not understand the long-term costs and benefits. Alter your equation until compliance is more rewarding than non-compliance.

Lost privileges for the casual child

The following example of lost privileges is one in which a child is not as aware of the costs and benefits of his behavior.

> Ben, aged 12, was casual about homework. He was certain that learning geography or writing five-paragraph essays were not necessary skills for professional baseball players—his future goal. His grades were poor due to missing assignments and projects. When Ben entered middle school he discovered that he was not able to play for his school unless he maintained a passing average in grades, which were given quarterly.
>
> In spite of impending doom, Ben did not connect missing assignments with the consequence of being cut from the team. His coach was enlisted to prompt Ben to complete assignments. Ben missed five minutes of practice time for every missing assignment. He had to have his missing assignments completed prior to playing games. In one situation, Ben completed his assignment on the bench, and then entered the game.
>
> As Ben worked on school work, his grades improved in a dazzling manner. Ben was amazed! He began to work for better grades, anticipating the rewards. His parents formerly paid for high grades—quarterly. Now they paid up weekly for completed assignments and high marks. Ben began to check the school homework site daily for any assignments that he had missed. He also liked to look at ads, deciding what he'd buy. More positively, Ben began to see himself as an academic success.
>
> After a period of success lasting several months, with just enough time for his parents to finally relax, Ben moved back to his former pattern, dismissing homework and long-term assignments. Baseball was over for the season.
>
> His parents simply used other positive experiences as motivators. Homework and chores needed to be done before time with friends, outings, or going to the gym to shoot hoops. They realized that Ben needed to have carrots and sticks.

Sometimes they did not have enough positive experiences to lever the negative. It was relatively simple to add them, using the same system. For example, Ben was finishing homework while his friend was texting to check on his progress. Ben's mother had arranged to take Ben and his buddies to the gym, knowing that he did not have his homework done. She picked up the buddies, dropped them at the gym, and then went home to Ben.

"How long until you are done with your homework? We are at the gym waiting for you?" the buddies texted.

Ben asked his mother, who held the phone until all homework was done, to text back. She wrote, "Ben's almost done. His parents won't drive him anywhere unless he has assignments completed."

After some adolescent protest, mostly aimed at the parent most likely to take pity and rescue him from consequences, Ben settled down to become a solid student. His parents said: "Why didn't we do this a year ago? Most nights we don't even have to remind him about homework. We sit down together once a week, posting the assignments' due dates on his computer schedule." He knows that his life will be complicated if he avoids his work. He knows that his life will be smooth if he does it."

Nasty words and friendly words, nasty and friendly buckets

Sometimes children use words in a hurtful way. If children are quite concrete in their thinking, I like to use two buckets. One is for friendly things to say when someone is angry, the other for mean things to say. Of course, we reward children with praise or something else positive when they are handling their frustration in a positive manner. If they use nasty words, tell them that they have to pay every time that they use words from the nasty bucket. The repayment can be a small chore for every hurtful expression, minutes towards an earlier bedtime, or a fine. Sometimes we have the offending child make the bed of the child who was offended, and so forth.

Restitution from children who lack assets— chores and family pawn shop

Some children need a strong message to stop negative behaviors. When parents are looking for leverage, the child manages to have no money, and is not of the opinion that they should have to make amends or make restitution. So, if the child does things like take their brother's allowance, or use their sister's new paints, they cannot easily re-pay. I like to give children the chance to make things right. If the child does not want to make amends, by doing his sister's chores, for example, parents can open a family pawn shop. An item of slightly greater value than the item lost is removed from the child by the parents. The child has a choice of making money for repayment, by doing chores, or losing the item. The parents take care of the business of paying off the person owed. This type of approach teaches all of the children in the family that the family is a fair one. The pawned item can either be given away or sold as used, depending on the parents' energies.

Stealing and taking things without asking

While we want to work on the moral aspect of taking someone's belongings, or intruding on the privacy of others, in the short term there needs to be an immediate consequence.

When it is a sibling issue, I allow a sibling to be taken to the doorway of the child who has taken items from the sibling. The sibling may choose an item to either play with for a few days or keep from the room of the sneaky child. The playing with or keeping decision is the parent's choice. Parents are the ones who enter the room, removing the item. This can lead to a discussion like this:

> "It's not fair!" says Ethan
>
> Gently, the parent says: "It feels really bad for someone to have your stuff, doesn't it? Your feelings right now are the ones that your brother felt when you took his stuff. Having it happen to you helps you to feel some of his feelings, stopping yourself next time. I'll do my best to catch you every time, making you pay your brother back. That way your brain will make the connection. You will figure out that you will end up feeling bad, not like a spy, when you sneak around."

I suggest starting with the earliest stages of conscience development: "I shouldn't steal because I'll get caught." Or, one level of conscience development up: "I shouldn't steal because others won't like me. I wouldn't like it if someone sneaked into my room, taking my stuff." Children understand those primitive ideas first. They are not ready for higher-level moral thinking until they have mastered these basic ideas.

Arguing

I suggest labeling arguing as just that: "That's arguing. I don't want to argue. When you calm down, we can discuss things. We may be able to compromise." Many of us struggle not to argue when we want our way, our timing. Children have not developed their abilities to tolerate frustration or shared attention. They are particularly prone to arguing as a pattern of conflict in the home.

The concept that we want to teach children is that their views are best heard if they are presented in a positive manner. The goal is to teach children how to use respectful voice tones and words. As parents, we want our children to present their views within a range of acceptable emotions.

There are exceptions when extra emotion is called for. For example, a child whose new birthday bike is being ridden for the first time—by their sibling! An outraged yell would be a forgivable reaction. But on a daily basis, we do not want to teach our children to be argumentative.

When children are in a squabble, parents can have the rule that the first person who quits, wins. For example:

> Hannah, aged eight, had a provocative steak. Alex, aged ten, argued back, holding his turf. Their parents said that living with the two of them was like being nibbled to death by a duck. When Hannah told Alex that he was eating his toast "wrong," Alex automatically said, "I'm not."
>
> "You are too." Hannah said. "I heard Mom say that you had bad manners."
>
> Taking the bait, Alex said, "When did she say that?" Then he remembered the rule, saying, "The rule is that the first one to stop talking wins. I win."
>
> Hannah said, "That's not true!"

> Alex grinned and went back to eating his toast.
> Mom said, "Nice job, Alex."

Parents sound like another child if they enter into arguments with their children. Debating or compromising is an entirely different issue. Parents can say: "Give me your point of view. But it does need to be given with respect." Having listented to their child's point of view parents can provide information or wisdom omitted from their child's conclusion.

> For example, Elise, aged nine, had gotten an award from school with a voucher for a treat from a particular chain store—but it had to be redeemed that day. She felt that she should be able to redeem it since it recognized her achievement. Her parents listened to her point of view. They said that they would have to compromise, since her sister had a sports match that night. Taking the coupon, the parents changed it to read that it was good for the next day, paid by the parents. Elise was able to calm herself. She asked, "May I invite a friend?"

When children are arguing to engage parents, I suggest that parents develop hearing problems. For example a parent can say, "I have closed my listening ears to that voice tone." Alternatively, "I have closed my ears to arguing children. I will listen to children whose voices are calmer. The first child who calms will get my attention."

Disciplining rigid and demanding children

Children often get locked into concrete, rigid ways of thinking about things. We try to teach them patterns of flexibility so that they recognize the potential of compromise. Some children are arguing because they can see only one potential solution. Writing down or discussing others will help them learn to be problem-solvers.

Things that help children to stop misbehavior include making plans for the day. When children begin to beg for take-out food, say: "What's the plan for the day? Oh, take-out isn't on the plan. However, we can add it for another day. What's our Thursday plan? Would it fit there?" Alternatively, parents can list something like fast food as an earned reward. They could say: "I'd love to get you fast food as a reward. What do you think you could do to earn it?"

Using "rock, paper, scissors" or a coin toss can be helpful when one person is going to be first, the other second. I strongly suggest that parents generally resist trying to keep score over who was first before, and who before that. It is wearing. On the other hand, it is great to have simple systems for limited issues. Children may want to have alternate weeks for jobs, for example. Perhaps one child washes the kitchen floor one week, and then swaps with another child to clean the bathroom the next.

Re-do

All of us do things that we regret at times. When children have behavioral issues, I like to ask them how they wish they had acted. Sometimes the consequence for children is a "re-do," doing what they wished that they had done. Children are much more likely to learn from doing the right thing, rather than hearing parents tell them what they should not have done. (Children with ADD or types of prenatal exposure will learn much better by doing the correct thing.) Sometimes I will simply have children's consequence be the "re-do" of the original situation. In order to cement the learning, we can have them practice the re-do two or three times, as in the following example.

> Jillian, aged nine, wanted her backpack, which was across the street in the car. She wanted to show her friend a new book that was in the backpack. Jillian's mother was busy talking to another person in front of the school. Jillian decided to retrieve the backpack herself, rather than asking her mother. "Watch this!" she said to her friend. She looked quickly up the road, crossed it, and pulled the spare key from behind the car license plate. She was delighted that it was where she watched her parents hide it. She got her backpack, flashed a smile of success to her waiting friend, and ran back across the street. A car horn blared as she scooted between the parked cars and crossed the road. Goal accomplished!
>
> Jillian's mother was at first too scared to speak. She had seen Jillian run across the street in front of a car. It was awful. Jillian's mother calmed herself, and then coached Jillian to think through the risks in the sequence. Then, she had Jillian discuss what she wished she had done. Jillian practiced asking her mother, waiting, and then crossing the road with

her mother three times. Then, Jillian had to come up with two additional ways she could have handled the situation.

Jillian's mother could have simply confiscated the item that Jillian wanted to show her friend. However, that would not have helped Jillian remember what to do the next time. Jillian's mother wanted her daughter to learn better checking-in with a parent, and better road habits. A re-do accomplished those goals best.

Processing sheets to help connect thoughts, feelings, and actions

When children have trouble connecting their actions, thoughts, and feelings, it can be helpful to practice with worksheets. In the example of Jillian, above, the mother wanted careful processing of the behavior. Processing sheets are a step further in helping children to understand their thoughts, feelings, and actions. The sheets avoid the "I don't know" responses that afflict some children.

This is an example of a worksheet for Janey, an 11-year-old child. She had difficulty with some friendly behaviors. She really wanted to do well, but had a tendency to want to get her own way without regard for the people who loved her.

JANEY'S PROGRESS TOWARDS BEING KIND AND HONEST

When did I want to be mean, lie, steal, or be sneaky today?

_____

_____

_____

_____

Did I lie, do mean things, or steal/sneak?

YES_____NO_____

If the answer above is "No. I did not lie. I was not mean. I did not steal/sneak," what happened that caused you to be so honest and kind? When did you feel like doing these wrong things, but did the right thing instead?

_____

_____

_____

Am I happy with myself for being kind or truthful?

YES_____NO_____

If I did something mean, lied, or stole/sneaked, what do I wish I had done instead?

_____

_____

_____

Who did I blame for my behavior when I was mean, lying, or stealing/sneaking? Or, what was my thinking or self-talk that made it OK? (Check the ones that fit, or write in the correct answer):

- ❑ They are not fair.
- ❑ I would not have to do this if they gave me what I wanted.
- ❑ They were mean first.
- ❑ I only steal from my parents or people I don't like, so it's not too bad.
- ❑ I'm mad at them (or someone) so I'm getting them back.

_____

_____

_____

What self-talk would have been more helpful?

❏ I don't like their rules, but I will obey anyway.

❏ I wouldn't like it if someone stole my things or lied to me. I won't do it to them.

❏ I want to be honest, not a liar.

❏ I am not in charge.

❏ My mom and dad love me.

❏ No one will trust me if I lie. I had better tell the truth.

Write a 100-word essay about what you did, why, and what you wish you had done instead. Write this on a separate piece of paper.

Write a 100-word essay. Describe how your actions changed the feelings between you and your parents. What are they feeling about you and what you did? How does it make you feel when you think about their feelings?

Write an essay about what you are going to do to make amends.

Share these sheets with your parents.

These processing sheets helped Janey to practice some more helpful thinking. She immediately began to improve at home, even though testing showed that she had brain-based issues getting the "big picture" in social skills. This strategy helped her to strengthen her weak area. She began to avoid the inevitable essays by stopping herself before she liberated money from her mother's purse or lied or hit out at school. Her parents were great cheerleaders, celebrating her successes.

Janey's school used a simple tracking device, with rewards. It looked like this:

FRIENDSHIP SKILLS AT SCHOOL

Check for "yes," leave blank for "no":

Keeps hands and feet to self—friendly hands and feet

	Mon	Tues	Wed	Thurs	Fri	Mon	Tues	Wed	Thurs	Fri
a.m.										
p.m.										

Talks politely to other children or ignores them if she's annoyed

	Mon	Tues	Wed	Thurs	Fri	Mon	Tues	Wed	Thurs	Fri
a.m.										
p.m.										

Keeps eyes on teacher—keeps her happy

	Mon	Tues	Wed	Thurs	Fri	Mon	Tues	Wed	Thurs	Fri
a.m.										
p.m.										

Answers teacher's questions (on topic)

	Mon	Tues	Wed	Thurs	Fri	Mon	Tues	Wed	Thurs	Fri
a.m.										
p.m.										

Person filling out form: a.m. _____ p.m. _____

Comments _____

_____

_____

_____

_____

_____

Please send this form home in backpack every afternoon. If parents have comments, they will add them and return the form. New form is used daily.

Forms like these are simple to adapt, depending on the child's needs. The school form is simple and quick for the teacher. Usually we use a reward system with the school form. It helps children to stay mindful when we use such forms.

Many children have to work on self-monitoring. The reward system helps to anchor the positive habits from self-control. The forms help them to keep thinking about appropriate behaviors. The first form, especially, helps children to notice when they are beginning to have "stinkin' thinkin'." All of us have selfish thoughts or reactions. When we notice ourselves having particular thoughts, we know that they will propel us into a downhill slide. The trick is to replace some of our thoughts with more helpful, and typically, more peace-loving, thoughts.

Parents may want to replicate these forms for their children, adapting them as needed. Sometimes it helps worn-out parents to have something like this that requires the children to do the work. Supervising or monitoring children's chores can feel like one more job for parents.

The first form puts the onus on the child, not the parents. Typically, you will want to withhold any rewards until the sheets are done. For example, no games, parties, television, play dates, desserts, or special activities until the forms are completed and amends are completed.

Lying

Almost all children will lie at some stage in childhood. If children are coming to you later in childhood, due to adoption or custody changes, lying is more to be expected. I suggest that parents think about the lying as a second-tier problem, with the formation of attachment being a first-tier problem.

When children continue to lie after they have formed attachment to you, typically they are either shame-based, or too afraid of possible consequences to tell the truth. Shame-based children feel so much shame that they do not like to acknowledge any of their mistakes. They are full of shame already! The children who are afraid of harsh consequences will have an automatic response of lying.

While my first emphasis in the home is forming some attachment, lies will ultimately interfere with attachment. A lie separates people from us. I like to talk about the lie as follows: "That is not something that I can believe. Think about it. I will talk to you about it later. You have a ten-minute grace period. You will not have a consequence for lying if you can tell the truth by the time the alarm goes off." Because some children will lie as their automatic pilot, we give them a little time to turn things around, telling the truth. When caught in a lie, most children will immediately argue in an effort to support their lies. Giving them a grace period stops this waste of time.

When children persist in lying, or in the "story," I suggest that parents react with an air of boredom. Pointing out to children the problems with their "story line" will only cause them to be more skillful liars as time goes on. Instead, say, "I'm no detective, so, I will have to go with the gut." The parent, with some dramatic flourish, turns the focus inward. "My gut says that you are lying or hiding something. You will have a consequence. Your consequence is…" (You will fill the blank with a job, early bedtime, a fine of money or loss of a privilege.)

The trick is to avoid getting drawn into an argument about the lie at this point. The child may very well want to fortify the lie. You have already won the round with an acceptable consequence. I strongly suggest that parents do not re-enter the ring for another round.

Some children will engage their siblings in these "who did it" wars. In this case, you can use the same techniques as above. Usually we have a pretty good idea as to the culprit's identity. I will suggest a coin toss. A parent says something like: "How would I know who did this? I'm not the police." At this point, I suggest flipping a coin. Assign heads or tails to children, then flip the coin. Influence your toss so that it favors the child who is likely telling the truth. The lack of control from the lying tends to demoralize children who enjoy lying as a form of mastery or a form of attention-seeking. Instead of gaining more control with lying, they have less control.

Many children persist in lying for the control that they feel from being "tricky." I call lies "mean tricks." When parents use a coin toss, children lose their sense of controlling their parents and teachers. They do not like the sense of unpredictability from the coin toss.

They also lose the drama of having the parent angry, flummoxed, and confused. The key for parents is to act matter-of-factly, ready to move on to more interesting parts of their day.

Videotaping and "fixing" a tantrum

Children want to do well. But while in the midst of a tantrum, it can be hard for them to remember techniques like "give myself a hug" or "deep breathing" as described in Chapter 3. Videotaping children can be a helpful way to teach them how to interrupt a tantrum. Parents can use their phones or a camera to record the tantrum. Later, parents can sit quietly with their child, looking at the tape. You can ask your child: "Where could you have stopped, using a calm-down technique? Which one would you have used?" I like to have children role-play what they chose with their parents. It helps them to remember the calming choice the next time that they are upset.

If children over the age of five years old are in the habit of tantrums, and are not interested in changing this habit, I often suggest as a consequence that they have to listen to their tantrum as long as everyone else had to listen to it. There is a strong caution on this. Sometimes children are having tantrums because something very bad is happening in their lives. For example, I have treated children who are having tantrums because they are being abused, or are seeing someone else being abused. Tantrums or "meltdowns" are common symptoms of distress in children. They are trying to signal that there is something terribly wrong. You want to be certain of your child's well-being before you began to assign consequences for their tantrums.

If your child has been abused, I would suggest about a year of calm parenting and some good therapy prior to consequences for tantrums. In the interim, parents can and should work on helping children to calm, to feel safe, and to put their feelings into words. There is no waiting time or end date for that support.

Plans for the day

The more difficult the child, the more helpful a plan for the day can be. (Similarly, the more difficult our day, as parents, the more helpful our plans may be!) The plan can be a series of pictures or a written list. The plan includes time for free choice, and possibilities for the choice.

Joshua, who was eight, had a daily plan. He was a little anxious, somewhat disorganized, and had a tendency to push limits. His plan settled him down, giving him predictability and focus. It was easy to produce and update daily on the family computer. It was printed out the evening before, and then reviewed before bed. Because of his age, he only had a few times on his list. His plan looked like this:

7:30 Get up and get a hug or snuggle.

Eat breakfast, brush teeth, wash face, get dressed.

Feed the dog.

8:30 Get backpack and coat. Get into car.

3:30 Home from school.

Eat snack and talk about day.

4:00 Unload backpack and organize homework.

4:15 Free time. Play outside or with lego pirate ship.

5:30 Homework time.

6:00 Set table for dinner.

Eat dinner.

Take out trash.

Free time with Dad. Ride bikes.

7:30 Bath.

Reading time.

8:30 Night snuggle and prayers.

Such plans help children to develop a sense of timing. Because the plans are written down, they are "set," so reduce the pressure on parents. Children think differently from adults. To a child, the written plan seems harder to change than a parent's mind.

Plans were described in the section on executive dysfunction in Chapter 3. However, they work well for anxious children during times of upheaval: moving homes, busy holidays, when family guests spend the night and when parents are traveling.

Eating, attachment, limits, and pressure

When we eat together as families, we have the chance to strengthen our attachments. We all hope for a mealtime that is pleasant and relaxed. After a busy day, parents can finally sit down and enjoy their children. But instead of enjoying our time, we may find ourselves worrying about nutrition issues.

- Did our children eat the correct amount?

- Did they get a balance from the right food groups?

- Should they be allowed to leave the table to go play when they hardly ate anything?

In spite of a reasonably good approach to eating, I found myself blurting out to my twig of a daughter, "You're losing ground! You're expending more energy than you are taking in!" She was reading with intensity at the table, legs swinging, and right hand drumming while eating raw broccoli for lunch. She was burning off calories faster than she consumed them! I recovered my logic when my daugther said, "You told me to listen to my appetite. Is your point that I should include some higher-calorie foods?" (It is always corrective when our kids sound more mature than we sound.)

Having a healthy model for eating and attachment greatly improves the quality of connection to our children. I found such a model through the Division of Responsibility (DOR). The DOR model was pioneered by dietitian and therapist Ellyn Satter. It is now the feeding strategy endorsed by the Academy of Nutrition and Dietetics. In this model:

- *Parents decide* the when, where, and what of feeding. (The exception would be infants, who are fed on demand, so they decide the "when." The "*when*" transitions to the parent through the late infancy and toddler stage.)

- *Children decide* how much and if they will eat from what is provided. Ideally food should be offered within enjoyable family meals, enhancing attachment.[1]

Feeding guru Katja Rowell, MD suggests that parents structure mealtimes so that children are secure in knowing when meals and snacks occur. Parents take the responsibility for selecting and preparing healthy food—including desserts. They offer balanced meals, not telling children how much to eat of which foods. When children choose from the meal offerings, the parents permit the choices. However, the parents do *not* allow grazing in between meals. Dr. Rowell strongly advises that parents let children come to the table with an appetite. The meals and snacks might be three meals and two snacks for children.[2]

If children have had a background of deprivation, I recommend that parents put out a fruit bowl or vegetable selection that will not unduly fill children up, but instead will give them a sense of food security. (The fruit/veggie selection should be simple and sufficient for the "tide them over" purpose.) If children say that they are "starving," parents can offer food to help them prior to a mealtime. But they should not offer an entirely separate meal.

> This transition from grazing to a plan was carried out by Janine, a parent with preteens. She said: "Just as I was preparing dinner, my kids entered the kitchen, opening a bag of chips. I know that they were hungry, but after they finished the chips, the meal just sat there. Our kitchen is a free-for-all."
>
> Janine took back her DOR jobs. She stopped buying large bags of chips. She realized that the after-school activities were leaving the children far too hungry before the meal. Since both children had endured food scarcity in the past, Janine did not want to restrict food when the children were so hungry. Instead, she began to supply a healthy snack at the time she picked up the children after sports. The children often had yogurt with berries and nuts. That way they did not have a seven-hour wait from school lunch to dinner, but a two-hour wait between snack and dinner. (Previously the snack had consisted of a piece of fruit and a drink carton, which was simply inadequate for two, rapidly growing athletes.) The

---

1   Satter, E. *Division of Responsibility.* Available through EllynSatterInstitute.org.
2   Rowell, K. (2013) *Love Me, Feed Me.* St. Paul, MN: Family Feeding Dynamics.

children still came to the table with an appetite. They began to help prepare an appetizer, talking to Janine while she finished dinner preparations.

The emphasis in the mealtime is to enjoy the experience of being together. It is an excellent time to talk, share feelings, discuss tastes of the food, and simply take pleasure in each other's company. As parents, we need to structure the food offered, and our children need to learn to listen to their bodies. They also need to develop a normal feeding pattern that allows them to develop an appetite. A parent's job is to provide healthy food, and to arrange mealtimes so that children's bodies stay balanced.

Recently, a parent complained that her son would say he was not hungry. She mentioned that he had eaten a yogurt and a sandwich as dinner was being prepared for the rest of the family. The roles were confused here. I suggested that the mother could have intervened, placing yogurt and the sandwich on the table at the same time as everyone else sat down to eat, telling him that she wanted them all to be together during dinner. Her choice, which she regretted, was allowing him to eat without the family. Her son was having trouble with connection. His choice to feed himself, eating alone, simply moved him in the disconnected direction. After talking to both his parents, her son agreed that he would eat with the family—as long as his parents prepared food a little more promptly. They all agreed, and things improved.

Dr. Karyn Purvis's work has shown that some children, after neglect or abuse, do better if fed a little every two hours. It keeps their cortisol levels in better balance.[3] This advice is excellent advice for children who are especially fragile. But even in these cases, the goal is to maintain pleasant mealtimes and a strong, positive association between parents and children. As the cortisol levels come into balance, then parents should be able to conform to a regular schedule.

Sometimes we buy food, and then complain when our children choose it. A father said to his son, "Why are you eating apple sauce— why not the apple?" It is helpful to question yourself in such a case.

---

3   Purvis, K. (2009) Texas Judicial Summit Presentation May 11–13, 2009. DVD available from TCU Institute of Child Development: www.child.tcu.edu.

"Why am I buying and serving apple sauce rather than apples?" Children with backgrounds of neglect or other medical conditions sometimes lack the muscle tone that allows them to chew and enjoy something crunchy like an apple. A feeding specialist (occupational therapist) could help develop these muscles.

Try these simple tips:

- Focus on behaviors, such as sitting down for meals, or not grazing.

- Have adequate and regular sleep. Lack of sleep is correlated to weight issues.

- Encourage regular and enjoyable exercise.

- Eat meals together, without comments on how much children are eating—or not.

- Stress interferes with body cues about hunger and fullness. Keep mealtimes pleasant.

- Children pressured to eat fruits and vegetables will eat less of these foods over time.

- Don't bribe or punish, beg, have them take two bites of something, or offer only new foods. Always have some food that is familiar on the table.[4]

Every day we have the opportunity for a wonderful experience of sharing food together, enjoying each other's company, and sustaining our positive connections. We want to limit wisely, so that our children are not thwarted in developing a healthy body image and healthy body weight. For more information on eating, I suggest the DOR website and the excellent book *Love Me, Feed Me* (Rowell 2013). Both are listed in the Resource List.

Summary

When we are teaching children to calm and limit themselves, and to care about daily responsibilities, we have the chance to bring out the best, or worst, in ourselves and our children. How children

---

4   Rowell, K. (2013) *Love Me, Feed Me,* p.41. St. Paul, MN: Family Feeding Dynamics.

react to limits and learning has a lot to do with their unique wiring. Some children and parents will have to work hard. Other children and parents will find that routines, school, and friendly behavior come easily. But no matter whether you and your child have an easy or rocky road, your relationship on the road can be companionable, warm, and hopeful.

Chapter 6

Life Stories

All of us have a story line about our lives. Our story includes a theme about how our lives work, as well as how our thoughts and feelings fit into the story line. We have explanations for the main events in our lives—even if the explanations are that we do not currently understand everything that happened to us. Still, we have a thoughtful approach to what we do not understand.

Our memories tend to be like the story boards in movies. These mental pictures show the main themes of our lives. They are the proof that the story line or theme of our life "movie" makes sense.

Parent story lines and story boards

When raising children, we parent them with quick reflections to our own story line. If you think that life works a particular way, and that feelings should be handled a particular way, then those attitudes show up in the way we react to our children. If we think that relationships are important, then we make time for relationships. We put aside our "to-do" list to show up, fully present, for our family.

When we are compassionate towards ourselves and others when thinking about our life struggles, then we show compassion and empathy towards our children. Painful experiences that have not been worked through tend to come up for us as we parent. Those painful or extremely shaming experiences will "pop" into our memories. They give us a disoriented manner with our children. We are likely to be angry, shamed, or afraid for no reason that our children can see.

When we spend some time thinking of painful events, or talking about them with friends or a professional, we "process" or "figure out and put away" these memories. They are not so vivid or disorienting. We are able to parent better. We are not overly upset or unsettled because of our memories as we deal with children.

People can have similar stories, but with very different conclusions or themes. If we think that life is tough and we can only count on ourselves, that feelings need to be stifled, and that only the strong survive, then we will raise our children with a hard hand. If we think that life can be tough as well as wonderful, and that all of us thrive better if we have people around us who care about us, then we will cultivate close, supportive relationships. We will tend to raise our children with a kind hand—so that they can come to us or other trustworthy people when there are the inevitable problems.

Take a moment, and maybe a pencil and paper, to think about your life.

- If we were making a movie of your life, what type of movie would it be?

- Would it be an heroic tale, one of a martyr, a romantic story, perhaps one of dedication to a passionate life cause?

- Where do your children fit into such a tale?

- What are the themes or beliefs that are part of the story?

- Do the "story boards" or the memories that you have, match your life story?

Sometimes the story boards and the world view turn out to be consistent and helpful.

One woman said: "I have always known that my gifts were to help others. I married a man with that same goal. We have been involved in non-profits that help with the needs of street people and kids in gangs. I also value self-care. I have to take care of myself or I won't be able to care for others. When our daughter had cancer, I knew that we would get through it. I was scared, prayed, and my daughter responded to the treatment. We are so happy to have this time with her. She looks great! She is likely to have another occurrence of cancer. But, I will enjoy the time that she is healthy. She beat cancer once. Maybe she can beat it again. It was very painful for her and for us, but we got through it as a family. Our friends were there, and I had our cancer support group. I know that God helped us."

In this example, the woman fully integrated the events of her life. She acknowledged both pain and joy. Her feelings were not overwhelming for the other four children in the family. Her world view was consistent with her life.

In the next case, the integration is absent.

> Eileen described the people in her family. She listed their accomplishment and the positive ways that they had shaped their community. She had a turn of phrase and a theme that things always "turned out for the best." But, the "story boards" included several instances in which she and other family members had been emotionally, or even physically, threatened. Warning signs about the danger of untrustworthy people were ignored. The family rule was to be trusting and optimistic. The optimism helped create successful careers and many close friends. The stories of being bilked and betrayed were treated with avoidance. Family members changed the subject with "but it turned out for the best."
>
> Eileen came for counseling after her sister's children had been exposed to a man who traumatized them. She asked: "Why can't the people of my family seem to avoid this type of person? Why are we so naïve?"
>
> She worked on integrating negative information, noticing warning signs, and putting up boundaries. Her gains allowed her to teach her children better boundaries and normal cautions. She dropped her "happy ending" viewpoint. "Since my sister and her children were traumatized, I see no happy ending. That false belief stops here."
>
> Her children continued the family legacy of optimism and positive social contributions in the community, but they reduced their risks.

As we parent, our intergenerational lives become apparent. As one man said: "My mother 'spoke' through me, pretty much raising my older son. With the next two, I had more to do with their upbringing. I sorted myself out enough to parent them instead of just doing what my mother did with me."

The "sorting out" process includes some consciousness about the big questions in life. A colleague mentioned that his parents were dreary. They always looked for what was wrong in life. His father had been terribly impacted by Hitler's scourge. He had to flee his country, making his way alone in his teen years. My friend said: "We had a depressing home life. We trudged through every day." In their life story, there was never a "before and now." Their life story continued to be negative. Something was always not quite right. While I do not want to be critical of a person who suffered so much, his legacy to his children was not one of celebration that he survived. He had depressed children.

That contrasted with a man who lived during the same time period, and who suffered many losses. "I was the only one of my brothers to survive and have children," he said. "Look at me now, surrounded by family. I married a beautiful woman, I have children and grandchildren. I have had a good life. I know what I lost, but I keep looking forward, not back. I know I'll see my brothers someday." He was grateful and generous, passing on a different legacy, a grateful heart, to his children.

When to get help with life stories

Thinking about how our life stories influence our children will cause us to improve on our healthy approaches and to work on our negative aspects. If you simply cannot think about events or times in your life without great distress, it is important to seek some professional help in order to make sense of those events. One reason that professional support works so well is because the professional is a steady, compassionate person who keeps people stable while they work through events. The professional basically "lends" their steady brain patterns to help those counselled to stay more stable as they work on emotional issues. Part of their job is to prevent the person being counselled from having their brain flood with too much painful emotion.

Children and consistency in what we say we believe

Some of the values that we have are in concert or contradiction with our life stories. All of us have inconsistencies. Many times we are happily unaware of these—both in ourselves or our society—

until our children point them out. Sometimes they tell us things that we do not want to hear. For example, "I'm afraid of you when you get angry." Or, "You give more attention to your computer than to me." Or, "You're always the last one to pick me up at day care. Do you like work better than me?"

In healthy families children will bring up these questions to their parents. While I want children to respect themselves and their parents when they speak, I do not expect them to have zen-like self-control when they are upset with parents or other family members. (I certainly do not have such self-control.) Anger is a predictable reaction when children's attachments are threatened in some way.

One of my children asked, "Why do you work on Saturday mornings when we are home from school on Saturday, and then you can't see us?" At that moment I thought, "Good question!" The initial reason for doing this, so that our children spent more time with us, their parents, and less in day care, no longer applied when our youngest child entered school. I changed my schedule promptly. Getting good feedback helps us to keep on-track in our families. I was so glad that my child spoke up.

When we have evident values in our families, our family members can question when we are not acting consistently with our family beliefs. Some *healthy* values are:

- Family comes first.

- Reserve your best time for your family.

- It's good to try hard things—even if you aren't always a "success."

- Be kind.

- Live simply.

- Be fair.

- Don't be selfish.

- Don't hate.

- Forgive others.

- Be polite.
- Reserve trust until you know people.
- Be respectful to others.
- No one is better than anyone else.
- Don't forget the poor.
- Don't spend everything you make.
- You don't have to buy everything that manufacturers make.
- Give back.
- Follow your passions.
- Work hard.
- De-stress.
- Have fun.
- Enjoy life.
- Suffering is part of life.
- Everyone makes mistakes.
- Apologize and try to make it up to people when you make mistakes.
- Show respect for everyone in the family.
- Share family chores.
- Work together.
- Be honest even if it looks like the dishonest are doing better.
- Pay attention to the feelings and plans of others in the family.
- Recognize differences and try to work them out.
- Compromise.
- You can count on your family for help.
- Love family members on purpose.

For people with a strong *spiritual* life, the values might include:

- Love God with all of your heart.

- Forgive in the way that you were forgiven.

- Love others as you were loved.

- Ask God how you should live your life and use your gifts.

Each family has a unique set of values and a hierarchy of values. Sometimes the story line produces a more *anxiety-driven* set of values for our children. Those values might be:

- Watch out.

- Don't trust anyone.

- It's a dog-eat-dog world.

- I will never let anyone hurt me the way X did.

- No one can look down on us if we own X.

- Appearances are more important than reality.

- Don't open that can of worms.

- Don't talk about a family member's mental illness.

- Don't talk about alcohol or drug use.

- Don't even try to talk about it—it will end in an argument.

- Your brother hit you—well, life's not fair. Try not to let it bother you.

- Males get more resources in the family.

- Females are sweet when they are helpless.

- Some races are better than others.

- I work so hard, and no one really cares.

- I do everything for everyone around here—I just want you to appreciate it.

When parents looked at the lists above, the reaction is always to head towards the healthy list. Sometimes we say that we believe the healthy list, but we mix in the anxiety driven one. When we try to give our children a belief system that says one thing, and then we expect them to live in another way, they will feel the tension. Life will not make sense. If we say that our family is important to us, but do not make time for our family, then our children will feel betrayed or confused. Or, if we say that our family respects all members, but we insult each other when we want our own way, children will feel angry. Children may be perplexed as to what to copy and what not to. *Usually people imitate the behavior, not the talk.*

Healthy role models

When parents have not had good role models, they can be heavy on knowing the values, but light on day-to-day behaviors that build healthy relationships. If you find yourself within that group, it helps to spend time with healthy families. Some people have borrowed grandparents, joined cooperative preschools, attended churches with support for families, joined community groups with activities for families, and so forth. The point is to spend times absorbing the behavioral habits of well-functioning families.

> Cherie, nine years old, was holding a toddler-sized baby doll in my office. She moved with easy rhythm, holding and speaking to the doll. Cherie used a brightened facial expression as she talked to the doll. Cherie was a miniature, ideal example of how to care for a baby. I was especially interested in this, since her life began with a year of orphanage care. I asked Cherie if she had been allowed to hold her baby sister after her sister's adoption.
>
> "Sometimes," she said, "But mainly I just watched my mother."
>
> Her mother said, "I had *a lot* of practice with my younger brother and sister." Mom's voice tones, body positions, and facial expressions had all been carefully recorded by Cherie. The mother said, "Cherie is already good with babies and children. Her cousins love it when she visits."

If you are not fortunate enough to be in such a family of "naturals," then I suggest looking for places to pick up skills and attitudes. A friend of mine, Terry, was an excellent parent. She volunteered in a developmental preschool in order to learn better ways of parenting. "My parents had a military background," she said. "Even among military families, my family was unusually strict. We were scared to make mistakes. I decided to learn some parenting skills before I scared my children."

Terry's life story line would have included a harsh time growing up, an honest recognition of her fear, her decision to raise her children in a healthier family, and then her decision to develop parenting skills before starting her family. Her "story boards" would have included the different people around her.

When there is something that does not make sense in our families, it can be easier than we think to make the changes. Sometimes we feel more "stuck" than we are. The "stuck" habit seems to come from childhood, when we were unable to make changes. As adults, taking responsibility for the quality of our lives is an important transition in our life stories. We can tell our children how we made these important changes. It gives children a template for the future. Children see the approaches that their parents use when making healthy choices. They also see the way in which people correct choices after mistakes or misfortune.

These discussions include the practical decisions as well as the "big questions." For example:

> Geoff, who worked in finance, was told by his boss to place a lower value on a business than was justified. The boss had a friend who wanted to buy the business. Geoff felt that he had already been asked to do things that were at the extreme edge of morality. This was over the line. Geoff sat down with his children, letting them know that he had to resign. "I will work hard to find a new job," he said. "In the meantime, we will need to cut back on expenses. I cannot be a cheat. I would feel awful in front of you, your mother, and God. Even if I didn't quit because cheating is wrong, I would have to do it for my reputation. If I got a bad reputation, I might not get jobs with good companies again."
>
> His family was very supportive—although a less-evolved child in the family complained about the loss of an expensive birthday gift that he was hoping for. One of the older children in the family said: "Dad can't be a cheater just so you get a mountain bike. He has to make better choices than that."

Interestingly, there is evidence that thinking about the "big questions" in life helps people to use higher-thinking centers and maintain mental acuity in later life. Our brains network in such a way that these thoughts strengthen the connections that keep them mentally vital.[1] Big questions include the following. "Why are we here? What is our meaning to each other as a community? How should people best help each other? How is our world changing and how am I changing with it? How do I pass on the best world possible to the next generation?"

Children's story lines

Children are developing story lines, or a belief in how life works, from an early age. As mentioned in Chapters 1 and 2, some of their first understanding is in the nature of their relationship with you. By seven months of age babies have a working pattern for you as sensitive and effective—or insensitive and unreliable. Of course, those patterns can change if you do. Or, if you are the new parent figure, children can find your pattern to be different from their former parenting figure.

It helps children who have more complicated life stories to have discussions and clear descriptions for the changes in their lives.

> Katie, a pre-teen girl, who had been moved abruptly first from her birth home, and then again from her grandmother's, as a toddler, said: "I thought that my parents might have kidnapped me. They never seemed to want to talk about my adoption. They said that my birth parents loved me and were just too young to take good care of me, but I felt that I was probably kidnapped. Like, that there was a bad secret. I had a scared feeling when I thought about it. I yelled at my mother that she wasn't really my mother. I have always felt like I was looking for someone else."
>
> This is an example of a life story that does not have enough detail to make sense for this girl. Katie's parents did not want to give dramatic details, which included an incarceration for bad checks, living in shelters and a van, and staying with relatives when the birthparents split up. She had feelings that did not fit the story line. When her parents went through the

---

1   Tanzi, R. (2013) *PBS Special: Super Brain.* Available on DVD "*SuperBrain with Dr. Rudy Tanzi,*" www.valleypbs.mybigcommerce.com/super-brain-with-dr-rudy-tanzi-dvd.

story with some details, she was able to make better sense of it. Her grandparents had wanted to raise her. She and her sister bonded to them. Then, her grandfather lost his job. The birth parents did not want their children raised with instability. They were no longer together, but were united in their decision: "We both have been poor our whole lives. The grandparents have a home, but not much more. We would like our kids to be in a family that could give them what we can't give them." So, they chose a couple who were financially stable, for whom their girls could be the only children.

"You were so scared when you came home with us," the adoptive mother told her daughter. I felt terrible for you. You couldn't keep your dinner down. You cried. You just had too much change, way too young." Her daughter cried, leaning into her mom. Her dad's hand was on her head. "We didn't want such a sudden transition. But, we had a terrible adoption worker who was pushing things. You weren't our child legally, so we had to follow her direction."

This is an example of a story line that makes sense. The facts and explanations helped Katie integrate events with feelings. The parents showed empathy. The "story boards" made sense for Katie. She did not like parts of the story, but it was no longer confusing and disorienting. "It's easier to obey them when I don't think that they are kidnappers, or that they didn't even care that I was scared," Katie said.

Not every story has such drama, but children and teens will ask for explanations for life events and values.

A teen girl was speaking to her mom. "Grandma makes a big deal about how good-looking people are, doesn't she? Was that really important to Grandma when you were growing up, Mom? You don't talk about looks. I saw some picture in the album. Grandma was pretty. You were pretty, too." The teen was asking about the difference in attitudes.

Her mother said: "Grandma thought that women would get better marriages and easier lives if they were good-looking. She didn't think that women would work outside of the home. The world changed and now most women have jobs at least some of the time. I raised you to believe that you should be able to support yourself, as I have. I don't know what your decisions will be like. But if you put a lot of attention on looks, you might undervalue other qualities that will probably be more important to your life in the long run. I thought that

Grandma overvalued looks with me, so I'm trying to do it right for you."

A father had the following conversation with his preteen daughter.

"You and Mom used to be so tense around each other," his daughter said. "Now you get along. Did I start doing better?"

The father replied: "We were really hurt and angry at the time of our divorce. We worked hard on healing up, forgiving each other, and doing the best for you. You're doing better, but you weren't the reason that we divorced, or that we started getting along better. We worked on being good parents to you. We weren't good at being married. But, we are good at being your parents."

In this story line, a child made her behavior pivotal in the story. This is typical for children. They see themselves as central, causative figures. One of the reasons that we discuss important life events with our children is to help them to correct these distortions. It helps them with a reality-based perception of life.

Summary

If children have a world view that is one of themselves as people of courage and passion, trying hard things, then challenges will be met with a mix of acceptance, strength, and perseverance. They will expect struggles and victories. If our children see themselves as powerless victims, then they will shape events to fit with that view. They will also be reluctant to try hard. Their view is that, after all, it probably will not work out anyway. Helping children who have had some early difficulties to find a "then and now" explanation will allow them to change their world view.

A teen said: "I lied and stole all of the time when I lived with my first mom. I loved her, but she would get drunk and would not even get food in the house. I stole money from her boyfriend's pockets to buy food for myself—and then lied about it. My life has changed. I need to be honest now. I knew that if I survived my first home, then I can survive anything. I have to trust my second mom and dad. They are trying to help me. I still want to pile up food and sneak, but it's just an old habit that I'm working hard to break."

Some people are main characters in a dramatic heroic tale. Others are martyrs in a painful slog towards the finish line. We tend to include or shape memories to fit the story line. If items are too painful, we might try to omit them. Our responsibility as parents is to help our children to have a healthy world view, and a life story that makes sense. After grief and trauma, people will need to alter their life stories into ones that include these realities. Intentionally including support for processing these feelings and the meaning of the events will provide a healthier world view—which includes optimism, healthy boundaries, and support.

Chapter 7

Promoting Attachment in Tweens and Teens

Teen years worry parents. Some of these worries are based on memories of our own teen years. We recall such a mixture of feelings! The emerging independence of our teenage sons and daughters means that they have the freedom to separate from us and our protection. Parents wonder if their teens will have good (or any) judgment. Will they be safe? Will they have good values? Will they stay connected to us? Will they do well enough in school to have a future? All of these are normal concerns for parents. Sometimes parents' worries can come across in such a way that teens' attachments are stressed at this age. Other parents steer a course that ends these years with parents and teens feeling close—with teens getting valuable help into adult years.

Knowing ourselves, developing our unique identities, is a process of seeing ourselves as separate from our parents. This work occupies teen years. It starts with a more realistic view of parents at about the age of 11 years old. Children realize that parents are not such superheroes, but have strengths and weaknesses. The process of identity formation continues throughout the teen years as young people decide how they are the same and different from their parents. They develop an identity outside their families. A challenge of this stage is keeping young people connected to their families as they spend increasing amounts of time outside their family by the end of the teen years.

In this chapter, we will discuss how to maintain positive attachments as youth are pushing away to develop their own identities. We will include concepts and practical "how-to" suggestions for teens and their parents. All of us want to keep attachments strong as our teens move up and out.

Secure attachments in teens

As mentioned in Chapters 1 and 2, attachments come in patterns, or styles, throughout the lifespan. Of course, the type of attachment that we all want is one that is secure—marked by trust, collaboration, and encouragement for exploration, giving us the sense that we are understood and "seen" in our closest relationships. Over the course of teen years our teenage sons and daughters begin to develop a more mature understanding about attachment. (Later-placed adoptees seem to mature a little later in their understanding of attachment, which makes them more vulnerable during this time-frame.)

What do parents look like when they are parenting in secure attachment relationships? Here are some examples:

- Parents use respectful speech and attitudes.

- Parents are sensitive and readily available for time and conversation.

- Parents have reasonable limits, and reasonably enforce those limits.

- Family routines are reliable.

All of these qualities help teens to either maintain or move towards secure attachments with parents. Parents who "hold their teens in their minds" giving teens the sense that they are seen, give their teens the intangible gift that they are valued and not alone. Teens are prone to feelings of loneliness and isolation as they separate their identities from their parents. Parents can help the process by making comments such as: "You're a unique person, different from me. I'm so enjoying watching you develop!" Teens, being teens, might respond with an "Ahhh" moment, or may just say: "That's nice. Have you seen my sweatshirt anywhere?"

Teens and their brains

Children do not have much abstract thought. This changes during tween and teen years. As sexual hormones hit the body, they begin shaping the brain into one that can use abstract thought. It makes our teens think about life differently. They no longer accept simple, concrete explanations. The teen who accepted the necessity of your limits one year, may argue persuasively the next. They examine our explanations.

Rather than taking the teen debates personally, parents can acknowledge that teens are using their new reasoning power. The glitch in the system is that most teens do not develop long-term perspective until their early- to mid-20s. While there are some early bloomers who are thinking long term at the age of 16 years old, most teens are not, and will not develop these concepts for several more years. They need our mature brains to supplement theirs. So, we need to strike the balance of treating our teens not as children, with concrete thinking, or as adults, with full, long-term thinking, but with abilities in between. They need us to protect their long-term opportunities, but also need to share in responsibility for decision-making along the way. We give our teens choices, but limit them. If your teen has executive dysfunction, which was described in Chapter 4, you will be especially hard working as a parent. Executive functioning develops through the mid-20s. Parents will need to keep young adults in their sphere of influence if they are still maturing in their executive skills.

> Maisie, who was a teen with executive functioning issues, *knew* that school was not for her. Using all available leverage, Maisie's single mother persuaded her to finish high school and to attend a few university classes. Maisie worked part time as an artist, and seemed oblivious to her career. At 21 years old her outlook changed. She decided that she *would* like to finish a degree. Motivated, she went on to teach and then design academic curricula. Her mother said: "I still don't know what happened. It was like she woke up."

This is a successful, but typical, scenario, for the later-developing teen.

Emotional skills

Teen years are great years to refine or learn emotional skills such as:

- seeing things in perspective

- understanding another's feelings

- learning to solve problems instead of avoiding them
- learning how to apologize or ask for an apology
- using calming techniques
- accepting responsibility
- connecting care of their bodies to their emotional well-being
- connecting their thoughts to their feelings, and then changing their thoughts to helpful ones to improve their feelings.

Parents are in a great position to teach these skills by describing their own emotions and thoughts. We do not ask our teens to take care of us, but do explain things that we would not discuss earlier in development. Most teens love a good adult drama, practicing their increasing insight. Family stories are great for teaching the lessons of emotional intelligence.

> A 16-year-old teen girl said, "I liked hearing about the way Aunt Kitty used *denial*. She just pretended her husband was great, but he was fooling around. I felt sorry for her, but it was *soooo* interesting! When my friend found out that her boyfriend was fooling around, I noticed that she was using denial like Aunt Kitty. They were both afraid to be alone. I remind myself not to use denial. I want to face problems instead. I broke up with my boyfriend who wasn't good for me."

This is an example of emotional intelligence (wisdom) that can be passed between parents and teens. If parents maintain a trusted, consultant role with their teens, they will be a source of emotional and real-life information. (And, it is a lot safer to learn from the mistakes of others than through our own mistakes, as in the example above.)

Hopeful, confident parents and teen tasks

Parents who are hopeful, caring, and confident about their teens will be attractive to their teens. All of us want to be successful in life. We want to move towards people who seem to promise that success. Parents can increase positive connection when they point out their teen's areas of mastery, competence, and increasing areas of maturity.

Wise parents watch the degree to which they threaten teens with a view of the world as a dangerous place. Teens with pessimistic, negative parents may decide that they need a better guide! Instead, parents should consistently teach teens how to stay safe through good decisions and the support of trusted others. Or, when there is danger, how teens should get help or get out of trouble.

Elise, who was 17 years old, was asked to participate in an outreach performance that would play for a downtown prison. She was the only female. "Mom," she said, "the guys in the band say it'll be safe. I don't think they really know for sure what's safe."

Her mother, who had been to the jail, described the location. Street parking was limited. The visitors' parking was in a rutted lot with no lighting in the rear half. Bail bond businesses were on three corners.

"If you walk more slowly, will the guys in the band know that they should slow down for you?" her mother asked.

"No," Elise replied.

"Have they thought how safety issues would be different for you, as a 105-pound person?"

"No," Elise replied. "And, even if I explained, they wouldn't really get it."

"How do you want to handle this?" her mother asked.

Elise said: "I'll call my friends. While I'm on the phone, I'll ask you if it's alright."

Elise called the band's leader. She called so the leader could hear her mother answer the phone, "May I go?" Elise held the phone away while her mother answered the question with a firm "no." Mom warmed to the task, spouting wisdom on safety—but realized that she was talking to an empty room. Elise had solved the problem. She used the conversation with her mother to help her assess the risks, which were high. She elicited her mother's firm "no," audible to her friend on the phone so that she did not have to argue the point with her friend. This case study illustrates the way that teens are using parents to the degree that they need. After Elise got what she wanted from her mother, she moved on to the next thing. (Her mother was dismissed in other words.)

Much of teen life, especially in the later years, seems to be like the example above. Parents are there when needed, but are dismissed when teens can handle things themselves. Parents with secure attachments to their teens are both safety nets and coaches for the high-wire act of teen years. Sometimes they are on the wire with their teens.

Tweens, teens, and parent moods

While everyone wants to be a hopeful, confident parent, the kick-off into teen years can be deflating. At about 11 years old, children start to develop abstract ability. Using that ability, they realize that parents are somewhat flawed and quite human. This tends to be a bit depressing for those of us who were the ideal a scant six months before. Rather than getting defensive, parents can make comments such as:

> "Your brain is changing right now. You are beginning to be able to think with a more adult-like brain. You'll notice my flaws now. But, I also want you to know that I am quite able to take good care of you. If you have questions about why I do things, please come to talk to me about it. I'd enjoy that discussion. I like how you think. I like to hear your thoughts." Those are words that bring preteens back into a close relationship with us.

Teens have both their changing bodies and changing brains to deal with. Nothing feels quite steady to them. In fact, they are not steady people. By 13 years old they are doing the necessary task of deciding how they are like and unlike their parents. (They seem to voice the "unlike" too much.) If teens have both birth parents and adoptive parents, they will have to do this identity work for two sets of parents, obtaining what information they can get about their birth parents to do the work.

Parents have a choice at this point. They can lend hope to their teens, pointing out these changes are normal. They show confidence that their teen will succeed in continuing to be a kind, good, and successful person. Or, parents can take very personally the moodiness of this stage, pushing their teen away when they are pushed. Parents who can enforce reasonable limits, but who sidestep control battles, do best at this stage.

Magic words from parents at the 13-year-old stage are: "I know that you are your own, unique person. Of course you would have different feelings and ideas from mine. I'm so interested in who you're becoming. I'm interested in your tastes in clothes and friends." These types of phrases let your teens know that it is fine with you that they are developing their own identities as separate. Yet, it strongly joins the two of you. Rather than feeling invisible, and misunderstood, they feel close and "seen."

Teens, challenges, and stress

Parents will need to monitor the stress level of their teens. Teens need challenges in order to mature, but the stresses have to be within their tolerance. Parents, who are a base of security, can help their teen with resources if teens need more support or if they are struggling. These include lessons in an area of talent, tutoring, mentoring, involvement in community groups, and ideas for handling stress that do not include completely avoiding it. As we move further into teen years, parents solve fewer of the problems, but remain as coaches and the final authority for their teens. They will "check-in" asking what help their teen needs. For example:

> Two teens could not figure out their school graduation requirements since both changed schools. The first teen, who had a secure attachment to her parents, said that she had the materials, but could not work out the requirements, since the courses had different names. She had tried to problem-solve with the school counselor, but failed. She and her father examined the materials together. Still confused, they went together to the school principal, looking at the requirements. It turned out that there was a problem that required a waiver for physical education. Physical education was offered at the same time as another required class. And, one of the classes had a name change since she began her program. The adults were able to both start and complete the waiver process at the meeting. The teen graduated on time.
>
> The second teen, who did not have a secure attachment to her parents, puzzled over the forms. She cried. She yelled, saying that that no one would help her. Finally, her father

looked at the paperwork. Already irritated by her emotional outbursts, he criticized her for waiting so long. He went to the school, embarrassed her in front of the principal, apologized for waiting so long, and then "solved" the problem by agreeing that she should attend summer school, taking physical education, and not graduating on time. "It's your own fault for putting this off," he said. "I hope that you learn your lesson from this."

Obviously, teens are much more forthcoming if parents are not shaming. It is to be expected that teens will have problems during teen years. These problems, and their solutions, become templates for them in learning how to solve life problems. We actually want our teens to have some problems so that they learn some problem-solving. During teen years, parents do best to treat teen problems as a normal part of life. Shaming is minimized, although teens are responsible for some of the cost of the solution.

Learning about close relationships

Teens increase their knowledge of close relationships as they observe the rhythms of relationships. They learn how people can have a hard time, get sad, become preoccupied, but come out of it within a couple of weeks. It helps them understand the processes of stress and how people can be temporarily, but not permanently, unavailable to each other. These templates are necessary for the ongoing complexities of relationships. It helps teens to be more emotionally steady in their own close relationships when they learn that parents have not emotionally abandoned them just because they had a few bad weeks at work. Emotional preoccupation can be temporary. Teens can also learn to ask for what they want in relationships with friends and family. A lot of these concepts are exercised by talking. While parents do not want to treat their teens as emotional peers, it does not hurt for them to know some of the workings of an adult relationship. For example, when I was working on a book, my husband told my teens that jobs would shift because I was completing the book. After I'd finished, the family could ask for me to be fully "present" again—especially in cooking for the family.

Teens learn a lot about reciprocal relationships through these years. All of us want our teens to have close friendships. While that is optimal, many teens are going through changes that will mean changes in their friendships. They switch friendship groups as they try out new interests or develop. Almost all teens deal with friends who are not loyal to them, or they hurt others by not being loyal themselves. Parents are in a good place to listen and to provide support as teens try to balance their own needs with the needs of their friends. Teens need to recognize when a friendship is one-sided, or when they no longer feel they have much in common with other people. If they trust us as parents, they will often come to us with questions about negotiating these changes in a way that is minimally harmful to themselves and their friends.

Of course, this usually includes romantic relationships. Teens have just as strong feelings as adults do in their romantic relationships. They feel intensely the joy or loss of a relationship— but their ability to commit or to sustain a relationship is lacking. It puts teens at special risk when in romantic relationships. Many parents wisely suggest that their teens put most of their energies into a steady, supportive group of friends. They also structure time spent with romantic relationships so that teens are still spending significant time working on their own achievements.

> A teen basketball player asked his girlfriend, "Will you come to watch my games?"
>
> She replied: "I don't know. I have to make sure my homework is done first. Usually it takes me a lot of time in the evening. I have to keep my average up to get into a good school."
>
> The boyfriend said to his buddy: "Basketball is wrecking my average! I like it, but I only decided to play it this year so I'd get a girlfriend. I might drop it since I have a girlfriend now."

This example is one of normal self-interest. It also reveals the limited decision-making that is normal for this age. Teens should be putting their own achievements first. There are few times in life that people have this opportunity. Teen years should be primarily devoted towards the teen's individual needs, not the teen couple needs. Since teens do not have much of a sense of time yet, it may seem to them that the relationship is long term. Parents can help with conversation and with clever maneuvers. For example, my husband once rented an exciting road race game when a too-serious teen boyfriend came over. The boy became completely engrossed in the game over the course of a few days. He was revealed to be much less mature than my daughter thought, giving her a different perspective.

All teens will need clear boundaries on curfews, as well as where they are, how they may be reached, and the nature of their activities. Also clear should be the enforcement of these boundaries. Usually these restrictions are loss of privileges and more home time or supervised time.

Securely attached teens look to parents for information and judgment when they feel that they need it. They tend to enjoy having the chance to handle some situations by themselves. As parents, we hope to see their relationships with friends become ones of trust, with some depth. It does not necessarily mean that they talk about everything, but there is evidence that they have strong connections with friends, as well as with us.

Less healthy patterns of attachment

While we have been discussing secure attachments, there are other patterns of attachment that are distortions of the optimal, secure style or pattern. This section is short, since the book's topic centers on creating secure attachments. However, seeing the patterns will help parents to curb a tendency to move into an unhealthy pattern.

In *disorganized attachments* there is marked hostility in the home—either between parents or with the teen and one or both parents. Criticism and shaming are prevalent in this pattern. Often there will be bizarre bits of conversation or behavior that just do not seem to make sense. There is a sense of something wacky "spliced" into the daily life. Sometimes teens are expected to look after the emotional or physical needs of their parents, especially in alcoholic families. Teens with these attachment patterns tend to have high rates of mental health problems.

In *preoccupied (insecure) attachments* teens are preoccupied with past losses and traumas. Unresolved losses in earlier life are strongly correlated with teen depression—and this can continue into the rest of adult life. In teens we see this trend clearly, often for the first time.

> A teen boy of 16 said: "I always feel that I'm less than other people. I feel that I lost something important that would give me confidence. I wasn't good enough for my mom to live. Don't tell me that it's not true. I know it's not logical. Why do I want to join her so much? It's like, 'What's the point?' It would be so much easier just to end it now. I would like to do it cleanly. I don't really want to hide my intent."

This is an example of a loss that led to clinical depression. The wounding of early losses and traumas often shapes the mood and the relationships that teens have at this stage. Professional counseling is such a helpful idea if this describes you or your teen. The strongly positive messages that people gave the teen, in the example above, simply did not touch this boy. He said, "I know that they say that I have all these great qualities, but it doesn't reach inside of me."

In *avoidant (insecure) attachment* patterns, the teen has decided that the parents are not available for emotional support. These teens shut down opportunities for emotional collaboration. There is a lack of trust in their relationships. They have determined that they need to be self-reliant, since others will probably let them down. These teens tend to look at their parents as people who are insensitive or unhelpful.

> A teen boy told me: "My parents told me that I had to be patient while they settled in my new foster brothers. I waited a year. Then, those boys went home.
>
> "My parents got my sisters. I waited another year. They were always saying, 'Can you just be patient for a little while longer? Your sisters need us.'
>
> "I used to think they were the best. I wanted to spend time with them. Now they are like, 'Want to do something together?' But I don't want to. They will just let me down again. I got used to doing without them. I don't want to try again."

This teen went from being securely attached to insecurely/avoidantly attached. He felt isolated and misunderstood in his home. His participation was marginal in celebrations or family activities. He planned a future with minimal parental contact. He did not use his parents' collaboration or support, except in emergencies. His parents perceived him as resentful when they pushed for a better relationship. But, when the teen tried to talk about his hurt, the parents became defensive. The course to a better relationship would have been for the parents to hear and respond to his hurts with tenderness. After that, they could pull him closer, and eventually ask him to improve his overall behavior towards them.

Teens form different attachment patterns with different parents, but one pattern begins to mark their own approach to close relationships over time. That is the pattern that they use in forming their own close relationships into the future. We want our teens to use a secure pattern.

Encouraging secure attachments

When we are encouraging secure attachments, we want to form an atmosphere in which greater independence on the part of our teen is met with support and enthusiasm. Their emotional pain is met with sensitivity. Their new ideas and experiences evoke a sense of discovery on our part. We allow ourselves to be changed and "updated" by the experiences of our teens. As parents, we want to take the lead in repairing our relationship breeches when things heat up or melt down. By "repair" I mean that we listen to each other's perspectives, take responsibility for the way in which we hurt each other, even if unintentionally, and then describe how valuable our teen is to us. All of the above require us to look and act like we have emotional and physical energy. We cannot be preoccupied and overcommitted if we are to do our job as parents!

A number of researchers and theorists have looked at the qualities of parents who are forming secure attachments, or maintaining secure attachments, during the teen years. This is what they have found:

- The parents are authoritative, but not authoritarian.

- They are warm.

- They are curious about their teen's views of the world, looking for opportunities for discussion.

- They negotiate when there is an opportunity for a joint project or a family decision—including a mix of ideas from everyone.

- They value the teen's friends.

- They set and enforce limits.

- They do not use violence or criticism.

- When the relationship is under stress, they respect their teen's emotions and respond to them.

- When teens withdraw, the parents do not withdraw. They remain available.

- They validate the teen's feelings of powerlessness, lack of value, or confusion when these feelings arise. They work to help the teen re-connect and feel valued again. They ask for better behavior after they re-connect, but not as a condition of re-connection.[1]

- The parents convey hope in their teen.[2]

Here are some ways that you can improve attachment between you and your teen:

- Increase the positive looping that teens have with you. That is, a back-and-forth that is only positive.

- Make zones of time that are completely positive. For example, mealtimes do not include a discussion of chores or homework. Or, the drive to guitar lessons does not include a discussion about the smell of pot on clothes. It will be addressed later.

- Touch your teen positively and often, if your teen permits this.

1   Johnson, S. and Lee, A. (2000) "Emotionally focused family therapy: restructuring attachment." In C.E. Baily (ed.) *Children in Therapy: Using the Family as a Resource*, pp.112–136. New York: Norton.
2   Diamond, G.S. (2005) "Attachment-based family therapy for depressed and anxious adolescents." In J. Lebow (ed.) *Handbook of Clinical Family Therapy*, pp.17–41. Indianapolis, Indiana: Wiley.

- Use food to entice your teen (and their friends) to associate you with nurture.

- Find new ways of connecting if you have fewer shared interests. Start a new activity with your teen. This might include volunteering at an animal shelter, paintballing, shopping, skiing, or getting or enjoying a family pet (mammal).

- Look for opportunities to have your teen's friends around, showing that you value their friends.

- Enjoy your teen's appearance. (Your decade and judgment in clothing really has passed.) On the other hand, do make certain that they wear "enough."

- Do not snipe at your teen or make negative, global comments. Keep a positive to negative comments ratio of 7:1.

- Have a life of your own. Do not make your teen's life your primary source of support or frustration. Get your emotional needs met elsewhere.

- Keep your marriage healthy, if you are married. Take time for romance. It gives your teen confidence in your family.

- Set limits, enforcing them with restrictions. Do not yell or carry-on in order to control behavior. Enforce limits by loss of privileges, or ask your teen to make amends.

- Apologize when you fail. Let your teen have the chance to forgive you or let you make amends.

Helping our teens, understanding our teens

The relationship lessons that we teach our tweens and teens are profound. In our secure attachment relationships we do the following:

- We teach our tweens and teens to get on the same emotional wavelength as others, attuning to them.

- We teach them the skill-set of connecting meaningfully with others.

- We guide learning how to understand our own emotions and interests, balancing these with an understanding of the emotions and interests of others.

- We show our teens how to handle stresses, using others to help us.

- We teach how to tolerate when people with problems become emotionally disconnected for short times, but come back to us.

Teens are learning about these realities as they develop a world view about attachment that is more complex. Our discussions in the home help them to put together a sturdy working model of understanding relationships.

When our teens have difficulties, many of us want to hold them too closely, causing them to be dependent. Alternatively, as parents, we might get hurt and act defensively when our teens have behavior problems. Teens need limits and support as they venture out, as well as parental approval and support as they encounter challenges. A lot of what our teens go through is *not about us*. It is our responsibility to make certain that they have the necessary support to weather challenges.

We want teens to have some problems. That way they will have real-life experiences in learning how to cope with problems before they leave our care. Most teens are not particularly skillful in dealing with problems at first. There is a learning curve. Wise parents allow teens to make decisions, and to have and solve problems, getting better at decision-making or problem-solving in the process.

A year before college, we removed the curfew on two of our teens. We wanted them to work on limiting themselves. If they were unable to do so, we stepped in, imposing the curfew again. However, in a few months we tried again. This way, they had real-life experience while they were still home with us.

We parents feel the urge to use our greater experience to prevent problems from occurring. It is better parenting to allow teens to fall into a few "holes" so that they learn the process of extricating themselves from a difficulty. We can ask them if they need a few ideas, or, we can actually intervene temporarily if the problem is too serious and outside their ability levels.

A teen's mood disorder, illegal activities, school failure, or a friend's threatened suicide would be in the "must intervene" category. Parents are intervening to protect their teen's well-being or future. The intervention should not be a rescue, so that the teen simply falls into the same hole again and again. If parents find themselves rescuing repeatedly, they need to obtain professional guidance. This is not a disgrace. It is a reality of our complex society. I recommend that parents obtain objective, professional counseling, if teens have learning, health, grief, trauma, or mood issues. Family counseling for parents is a good idea so that the parents can get on the same page.

Allowing lessons from negative experiences

Many teens with executive dysfunction or attention deficit disorder (ADD) learn best from experiences. Our words may pass them by. This is hard on parents. Naturally, we want to save our teens from painful consequences. It is not a moral problem that they have ADD. But you have to begin the process of letting them learn lessons from behavioral consequences. Examples are getting a poor grade by putting off a homework assignment, missing the team bus and a game because their sports equipment is missing, or losing a friend because of impulsive comments.

You may want to allow some of these losses, even if you could swoop in to "save the day," so that your teen feels the negative effects of their actions. The proper attitude is a compassionate, kind reflection that the teen will eventually be able to foresee negative consequences. (Inhibit the desire to trumpet, "I told you that things like this would happen if you wouldn't listen!") Your teen needs support and encouragement in order to try again and try differently. This would be the time to lend a little hope and encouragement.

Of course, you do not seek out disappointments, blaming the teen for their brain-based problem.

If there is a natural solution, parents would not want to "set up" their teen for a disappointment.

A parent of a teen with ADD found a permission slip for the all-day event that concluded Junior High. The parent mentioned that she found it in the laundry room, and that it needed to be signed and turned in that day. "Thanks, Mom. It would be so awful to miss that!" her teen said. "I am trying to think how I could remind myself so that I don't forget important things." That led to a discussion on using a cell phone reminder.

The balance is to keep enough support that your teen feels optimistic about life, and shows successive improvements in handling life challenges.

Some teens begin to sink during these years. Because issues like depression, obsessive compulsive disorder, and anxiety may gain traction at this stage of development, parents should be more concerned with diagnosis than teaching lessons. If your tween or teen is developing a mental illness at this stage, your efforts should be put into handling that mental illness. Parents should not embark on teaching a series of lessons before they understand their teen's state of mind.

Tough love, applied to a depressed teen, can be catastrophic. I counselled a 13-year-old whose teacher was planning to restrict his attendance at the school holiday party due to missing assignments. In fact, the boy was planning suicide for that weekend. Fortunately, the parents and I were able to help this boy, who is doing well today. However, the timing of the teacher's consequence would have been awful. As it was, a quick note to the teacher allowed for some flexibility. The boy eventually recovered from depression and did much better at school.

Connection and encouragement

Our teens need us when they need us. They seem to be self-sustaining—until they are not. They do not schedule their neediness. At our house, some of our critical, later-teen conversations went like this: There would be a knock at our bedroom door—usually just after my husband and I had settled in bed. We turned on the light, calling, "Come in." Our teen would apologize and suggest leaving. (They always seemed surprised that we were in bed.) But we would act like it was perfect timing. "We weren't asleep yet. It's fine." Then, our teen would talk to us about something quite significant. (I seem to remember a slight humming in the air, as if there were an electric charge present.) I would know that how we listened would be *very important...*

Teens need continued regular connection with their parents. They need lots of positive comments about their emerging identities. They can benefit from your continued help coaching "self skills" (calming, planning, perspective-taking, insight, trying again). As parents, we make ourselves available for being consultants on some of the emotional challenges that our teens face.

At our house I found that cooking on Saturday morning was an ideal time to make myself available. I would make soup and bake. Our teens would wake up slowly, arriving in the kitchen to talk. They ate and we talked together while I cooked. It was an easy-going pajama time that continued during school breaks after they left home. Those were great opportunities to connect and to enjoy each other.

But while we want to make ourselves available, we also want to give our teens the chance to solve some relationship problems themselves. The statements sound like: "You may want to solve this problem yourself between your friend and your boyfriend. I'll be interested in what you're thinking. If you need someone to bounce ideas off, then let me know." You can also give hints, clues, or sample suggestions. (Your suggestion is typically *not* the one chosen.)

Effective parents are able to:

- enhance dreams

- encourage areas of mastery

- help teens to develop insight into their thoughts and feelings as well as insight into the feelings of others

- enjoy their teens

- notice when their teens need limits, providing limits

- give reasonable and effective consequences when teens ignore limits.

They do not do the following:

- lecture

- forecast doom with no solution

- refuse to consider compromises or new ideas

- act harshly

- diminish family members in order to gain dominance

- behave violently either psychologically or physically

- waffle on about consequences or limits when teens have defied or ignored limits.

When teens and families are in difficult times

If teens are moving into danger areas, then parents will need to provide tighter limits, increased structure, and an insistence that the teen pays for the cost or inconvenience of their negative behaviors. However, the parents continue to be caring, ready for connection, and considerate of their teen's feelings. The message is loud and clear that their teen's well-being, rather than the immediate problem, is most important to parents. Wise parents slow down, proceeding carefully and with a steady hand, when their teen has troubles. They are not rigid, mean, and distancing.

Some parents will see the clear outlines of depression or anxiety in these years. Or, they may notice that their teen has particularly low self-esteem. Especially in schools where students are constantly being compared to their peers, teens with academic struggles are at-risk for low self-esteem. They may start to compute their grade point average as their worth. Parents should be aware that teen suicide is a leading cause of death for this age range. Any threats should be taken seriously. If things are simply not going well, medical check-ups and mental health assessments should be arranged.

> One boy entered teen years feeling good about himself. His family began having difficulty feeling close to him as he began to suffer from obsessions and depression. His friendships moved to an alternative crowd and grades deteriorated. He was reluctant to tell his parents that he thought he was going

crazy. With strong parenting support, he eventually revealed his problem, which was genetic and affected other family members. Over several years he found the strength and skills to deal with these issues. The parents said: "We are so grateful that we stayed supportive, even when we did not understand. If we had gotten tough, we don't think he would have made it. He's a joy to be around now. He's a caring young man."

When you do not seem to understand changes in your teen, a prudent course is to contine to be steady and sensitive. It is not a time to move into a tough approach.

All parents want their teen to enjoy a positive identity. Things that help teens to develop this type of self-confidence are:

- secure parental attachment

- positive influence of other adults

- acceptance in a peer group

- areas of mastery

- good ethnic identity.

If your teen is having difficulties, looking at the ways that you can help your teen in some of the areas above will be important. Sometimes a mentor can help your teen more than you are able to. If your teen is experiencing loneliness or rejection daily, then look for a place where the teen can learn some relationship skills. Sometimes teens are simply in a no-win situation for them. A teen who was the only person of her ethnicity in a school, said to her parents: "I don't know what you were thinking! I get teased by other kids on the way to school, have to take two buses to get there, and always feel like an outsider." Her self-esteem was immediately improved by moving into a racially integrated school.

Teens may not want to speak to their parents if there is a pattern of conflict. They say, "All that happens is that we end up fighting anyway." They will retreat into their rooms so that they avoid conflict. This is a great time to get some family therapy. When I was working with a family, a teen learned to listen to her mother, without interrupting, and vice versa. I prompted them to listen with respect. The teen said: "We actually worked it out! We could do that at home if we needed to." My job was to keep them both calm enough to keep talking and listening. It was a simple step, needing just two office visits to accomplish.

At times it seems as if our teens want to fight with us. (I am sure they feel the same.) It is critical for parents to continue to put in the effort to communicate, without comebacks or lecturing. If you feel yourself being baited, you can respond by saying: "I value being with you so much, that I'm not going to respond to that. I'd rather just hang out with you. I've missed being with you." Even if they grumble and move off, at least you have left a positive comment in the air. Often teens will re-emerge saying, "Actually, I had a horrible day..." They may even apologize for trying to involve you in an argument.

Parents who respond sensitively to their teens, and who make statements about the teen being "an important member of the family," find that they have the best chance of keeping a close relationship with their teen—in spite of any hard times through the teen years.

Parent failures and apologies

If you are a parent of a teen, you may have finished the sections above thinking, "I am a terrible person and parent—I have blown this." Join the club. We all find ourselves doing exactly the opposite of what we should be doing some of the time in these years. I believe that if you cannot model the correct behavior, at least you can model a good apology.

A good apology is not an explanation. That may come later. An apology sounds like:

- "I am sorry that I was sarcastic."

- "I am sorry that I yelled at you."

- "I am sorry that I used that tone."

- "I am sorry that I didn't listen to your point of view."

Perhaps you over-reacted. The apology would be, "I'm sorry that I did not trust you." It can include, "Would you give me another chance to listen to you?" Or, "Your feelings are important to me. Is there some way that I can show that to you now? I'm sorry that I didn't listen before."

Teens will usually describe how they felt at that point. It is best to resist butting in as they describe how you wounded them. Usually we feel defensive, so jump in to defend ourselves. Instead…listen. Say that you are sorry again if you need to. Sometimes teens will forgive easily, and sometimes it will take a while. It depends both on the teen and on the gravity of the situation. Offering especially good food tends to be an extremely successful move on the parent's part during an apology period.

After things are better, or, if it is important for teens to know why we behaved as we did, we can describe why we had trouble. This is not given as an excuse, but as an explanation. Explanations include things that made you take such a poor turn in the road. "I just got back from the hospital, visiting my sick relative, to find a message from your school that you weren't in school today."

Another example:

> "I found out that you went to a party at the Smiths that I asked you not to attend. Earlier this year the Smiths allowed drinking at one of their parties. One of the kids who attended was drinking, had a car accident, and was jailed. I was scared and angry to think that you would be at that party. I should have asked you about it, rather than accusing you. Later, I found out that you only stopped to pick up a friend there, and then left before the party got going. But, I was scared and acted from that fear."

Sometimes your teen has done the wrong thing, but you also handled it poorly. You may have to give a consequence, but apologize for the way you came across. For example:

> "You drove without a license, just with your permit. We weren't home. You took the car without permission. I'm sorry that I yelled at you and that I told you that I couldn't trust you. I should have handled this better, hearing your side of the story."
>
> After the apology the parent says: "We're putting off your driver's license for another six months. Your friend pressured you to drive him to work so that he wouldn't lose his job, saying, it was only four miles. I found out after listening to you that your friend's mother, who has a license, went with you.

But we were clear that you weren't to drive the car while we were gone. I think that you need time to be able to avoid caving in to friends' pressures. We don't think that it's safe to have you driving teen friends. You'll be tempted to lie to us rather than disappoint your friends. I don't want you in that situation. I love you and don't want you to end up hurt in an accident."

If you feel very upset by your teen, it is just fine to say, "I am upset right now, and need some time to think about this clearly." You do not have to wait until you show zen-like control. Rather, you want to be able to speak with respect, even if you are angry and disappointed in your teen.

Summary

Parenting our teens is not done by formula. It is a dynamic connection with amazing young people—who soon will be making decisions for our society. Our day-to-day living can be as up and down as the moods of our teens. Rather than shaping them so that they best fit into our homes, we shape them so that they are their best selves, finding their place in the world. It is an amazing privilege to parent teens and to enjoy them. At the end of this stage, we know our teens as caring, perceptive people who have the capacity to understand themselves, other people, and to use this understanding as they move into society. That they choose to keep a relationship with us is a gift, more than what we could have deserved.

EPILOGUE

I wrote this book filled with amazement at the power of relationships. Researchers prove what our storytellers and songwriters have always known—in our attachments we become our truest and best selves.

I wrote the book with a sense of looking backwards—over a 30-year career working with attachment, and over a long parenting journey. Today, as I finished the book, one of my daughters sent me an email. She has significant health issues, but applies the wisdom from secure attachment: "I want to thank you for teaching me my own value, that I'm as good as anyone, and never lowering my expectations. That strength of spirit and trust in myself has allowed me to create and enjoy the life I have."

Another daughter, coincidentally, finished her doctoral thesis the same day. She emailed me, celebrating that she had completed her writing. Both women are confident adults, each uniquely gifted, operating in the strength of their gifts.

All of us, as parents, want to equip our children to be strong, moral, compassionate, and joyful adults. Knowing that troubles are sure to come into every life, we want to include the makings of resiliency in our children's upbringing. I enjoyed weaving the essentials of resiliency into the pages of this book.

Through our secure attachments we lay foundations of security and resiliency for our children. We also raise adults to be compassionate contributors to the overall good, caring for their brothers and sisters on this earth.

RESOURCE LIST

Organizations and websites
US
ATTACh
Website: www.attach.org

This international organization helps parents and therapists when children are having significant difficulties with attachment. It publishes a "white paper" position on which therapies are considered helpful, and which are coercive and probably harmful.

BeeVisual, LLC
Phone: 508 229 0500

Website: www.beevisual.com

This is a website with apps that help children to get and stay organized, and to learn and use social skills. Children are able to use tablets, phones, or computers with the applications.

Center for Cognitive-Behavioral Assessment and Remediation
Website: www.bgcenter.com

This is a website run by developmental psychologist Dr. Boris Gindis. It has many articles useful for educational planning, and is not exclusively for those adopted from Eastern Europe.

CHADD—Children and Adults with Attention-Deficit/Hyperactivity Disorder
8181 Professional Place, Suite 201
Landover, MD 20785
Phone: 800 233 4050
Phone: 301 306 7070
Fax: 301 306 7090
Website: www.chadd.org

This organization is a powerhouse with information about education, medication, home routines, counseling, and local support groups. Gives invaluable information to advocate for school planning.

Child Welfare Information Gateway

Website: www.childwelfare.gov

Child Welfare Information Gateway provides access to information and resources to help protect children and strengthen families. Gives information about all aspects of adoption and about child abuse and neglect, including publications, referrals to services, and searches of its computerized information databases. A service of the Children's Bureau, Administration for Children and Families, U.S. Department of Health and Human Services.

Child Trauma Academy

Feigin Center, Suite 715
Texas Children's Hospital
6621 Fannin
Houston, TX 77030

Website: www.childtrauma.org

This is an organization that produces sound, practical educational materials for parents and caregivers, giving them access to work by some of the finest calibre professionals. Materials are composed or edited by Bruce Perry, MD, PhD, a psychiatrist and world expert on children's track development and trauma.

FASD: Families Moving Forward

Dr. Heather Carmichael Olson
2001 Eight Ave. Suite 400
Seatle, WA 98121
Phone: 206 987 7581

Website: http://depts.washington.edu/fmffasd/home

This is a website, with resources, to help children with FASD (fetal alcohol spectrum disorder). The organization is excellent in supporting entire families.

Fostering Families Today

Website: www.fosteringfamiliestoday.com

The magazine *Fostering Families Today* published by Louis & Co (publishers of *Adoption Today*), is packed with sound and well-written articles, and is graphically attractive as well. It is also helpful for later-placed adopted children. It is one of my favorite resources in the field.

FRUA—Friends of Russian and Ukranian Adoption (including Neighboring Countries)
PO Box 2944
Merrifield, VA 22116

Website: www.frua.org

This organization is a powerhouse. Join and sign up for their Family Focus newsletter, and make use of their dynamic online discussion group. Better yet, go to or order tapes from their national conference. You do not have to have adopted from Eastern Europe to appreciate these resources.

Kinship Center

Website: www.kinshipcenter.org

This is a great source for adoption-related information. Sharon Kaplan Rosia and her colleagues are the inspiration behind these materials, covering important aspects of parenting and professional support.

Model Me Kids

Website: www.modelmekids.com

This is a website that sells DVDs for children who are learning social skills. It is great as a teaching tool for families or for schools. It is suitable for children after neglect or for children with autism.

National Child Traumatic Stress Network

Website: www.nctsn.org

This is an excellent group with support for foster or adoptive parents who are parenting children who were traumatized. The website is excellent: parent friendly for parents, and practice rich for therapists accessing it.

National Council on Adoptable Children (NACAC)
970 Raymond Avenue, Suite 106
St. Paul, MN 55114-1149
Phone: 1 800 470 6665

Website: www.nacac.org

This organization has legal, ethical, and social work practice influences on children's adoption issues. It is a powerful advocacy organization and leads in improving adoption practices.

Pact, an Adoption Alliance
3450 Sacramento Street, Suite 239
San Francisco, CA 94118
Phone: 425 221 6957
Fax: 510 482 2089

Website: www.pactadopt.org

This is an adoption placement and education service focused on placing children of color and supporting families raising adopted children of color either in-racially or transracially.

Sensory Processing Disorders

Website: www.sensory-processing-disorder.com

This is a great website for parents whose children may have sensory sensitivities. It has a checklist and a series of actions to take to help your child.

Sibshops

Website: www.siblingsupport.org

The sibling support project has developed an international directory of these workshops designed to best support siblings of special needs children. The kids love them.

Society of Special Needs Adoptive Parents Newsletter
Phone: 604 687 3364
Email: snap@snap.bce.ca.

Website: www.snap.be.ca

This provides the latest on special needs issues, including FASD (Fetal Alcohol Spectrum Disorder). It is extremely practical. SNAP also has a great, downloadable book on parenting children affected by FASD.

UK

Adoptionplus
Moulsoe Business Centre
Cranfield Road
Moulsoe
Newport Pagnell
MK16 0FJ
Phone: 01908 218251
Email: Enquiries@adoptionplus.co.uk
Website: www.adoptionplus.co.uk

Adoption UK
Linden House
55 The Green
South Bar Street
Banbury
OX16 9AB
Phone: 01295 752240
Website: www.adoptionuk.org

BAAF (British Association for Adoption and Fostering)
Saffron House
6–10 Kirby Street
London
EC1N 8TS
Phone: 020 7421 2600
Email: mail@baaf.org.uk
Website: www.baaf.org.uk

Family Futures Consortium Ltd
3–4 Floral Place
7–9 Northampton Grove
Islington
London
N1 2PL
Phone: 020 7354 4161
Email: contact@familyfutures.co.uk
Website: www.familyfutures.co.uk

Canada
Adoption Council of Canada
The Adoption Council of Canada
211 Bronson Avenue
Mailbox #231
Ottawa, Ontario
K1R 6H5

Canada Adopts!
Email: info@canadaadopts.com
Website: www.canadaadopts.com

Australia
Australians Caring for Children (ACC)
PO Box 7182
Bondi Beach
NSW 2026
Email: info@accau.org
Phone: (612) 9389 1889
Website: www.accau.org

Fostering and Adoption Services
161 Great Eastern Highway
Belmont WA 6104
Postal address: PO Box 641
Belmont WA 6984
Email: info@adoptions@dcp.wa.gov.au
Phone: (08) 92593414
Website: www.childprotection.wa.gov.au

Books and DVDs for adults and for children

All About Adoption by Marc Nemiroll and Jane Annunziata (Magination Press, 2004).
   This children's book for ages 6–11 includes good information about children's feelings, adoptive families, and birthparents. It also covers anxiety, older child adoption, and birthparent issues.

Attachment in Common Sense and Doodles: A Practical Guide by Miriam Silver (Jessica Kingsley Publishers, 2013).

This book describes attachment issues in a clear and understandable manner.

Belly-Breathing. Available at www.buildingblockstherapy.com/belly-breathing-with-elmo.

This is a fun video for kids. It demonstrates how to do deep breathing, or belly-breathing.

The Best Single Mom in the World: How I Was Adopted by Mary Zisk (Albert Whitman and Company, 2001).

Want a cheerfully illustrated read-aloud book for a single-parent family? This is it.

Child with Special Needs: Encouraging Intellectual and Emotional Growth by Stanley Greenspan and Serena Wieder (Addison Wesley, 1998).

Sophisticated parents or professionals will appreciate this approach, which stimulates development.

A Child's Journey Through Placement by Vera Fahlberg, MD (Jessica Kingsley Publishers, 2012).

This beautifully written book is a treasure for professionals who are placing children or raising children. Dr. Fahlberg's wisdom and sensitivity shine through.

Connecting with Kids through Stories by Denise Lacher, Todd Nichols, and Joanne May (Jessica Kingsley Publishers, 2005).

This book employs storytelling to help children to change their narratives and schema of life. It is a helpful guide for parents and clinicians.

Creating Capacity for Attachment by Arthur Becker-Weidman and Deborah Shell (eds) (Wood and Barnes Publishing, 2005).

This book is a lovely addition to the literature. It helps clinicians to develop their practice skills in areas of assessment, attunement, and treatment for children with attachment issues.

Creating Loving Attachments, Parenting with PACE to Nurture Confidence and Security in the Troubled Child by Kim Golding and Daniel Hughes (Jessica Kingsley Publishers, 2012).

I so enjoyed the emphasis on nurture and play in this book. The book is written for sophisticated parents, or parent professionals. It helps keep parents sensitive and communicative, and is especially good for children in late elementary years and up.

Delivered from Distraction: Getting the Most out of Life with Attention Deficit Disorder by Edward Hallowell and John Ratey (New York, Ballantine Books, 2005).

This book is a guide for many aspects of life. It is great for families with a member with attention deficit disorder.

Executive Skills in Children and Adolescents by Peg Dawson and Richard Guare (Guilford Press, 2010).

This is a workbook with templates that help your teen to plan and organize their school projects, their rooms, and their time. Invaluable!

Fostering Changes: Myth, Meaning and Magic Bullets in Attachment Theory by Richard Delaney (Wood and Barnes Publishing, 2006).

This book describes good techniques and an updated theoretical base as a way to help older children in foster homes. The book is practical and respectful.

Growing an In-Sync Child by Carol Kranowitz (Perigee, 2010).

This is another practical book to help children move beyond the limits of sensory sensitivities. This is the latest, following the *Out-of-Sync Child* and *The Out-of-Sync Child Has Fun*. This author demystifies sensory sensitivities and teaches how best to parent children who have them.

Helping Adolescents with ADHD & Learning Disabilities: Ready-to-Use Tips, Techniques, and Checklists for School Success by Judith Greenbaum PhD and Geraldine Markel PhD (Jossey-Bass, 2001).

This book is great for giving ideas for Individualized Education Plans and school meetings. It helps parents and teens in school matters.

Inside Transracial Adoption by Gail Steinberg and Beth Hall (Jessica Kingsley Publishers, 2013).

This book explores the complexities of transracial adoption while equipping parents with practical and compassionate advice. To top it off, it is a good read!

Help is on the Way—A Child's Book About ADD by Marc Neniroff and Jane Annunziata (Magination Press, 1998).

This is a fun and readable book to use with children who have been diagnosed with attention deficit disorder.

The Mulberry Bird by Anne Braff Brodzinsky (Jessica Kingsley Publishers, 2012).

Children who are in elementary school like this book. It is particularly helpful to children who have a history of poor care. The children use the metaphors to talk to parents.

The Mystery of Risk by Ira Chasnoff (NTI Upstream, 2011).

This is a great book for parents whose children were prenatally exposed to alcohol and/or drugs. Ira Chasnoff gives clear information about brain functioning after exposure and how to bring out the best in children.

Navigating the Social World by Jeanette McAfee (Future Horizons, 2002).

This is a handbook for children who have difficulty with social relatedness. It includes exercises to build these capacities in the older child. I have had great success using this in a guided way with college-age coaches and my preteen clients.

No Mind Left Behind: Understanding and Fostering Executive Control by Adam Cox (Perigee Press, 2008).

This is an outstanding book for parents who are developing executive functioning in their families. The book's tone is positive and the suggestions are solid.

Parenting Children Affected by Fetal Alcohol Syndrome—A Guide for Daily Living by the Ministry for Children and Families, British Columbia.

Available as a free downloaded book from snap@snap.be.ca. It is a regularly updated and extremely practical guide to daily schedules as well as approaches that work with prenatally exposed infants, children, and teens.

Parenting from the Inside Out by Daniel J. Siegel and Mary Hartzell (Penguin/Putnam, 2003).

This excellent book explores building family relationships in a brain-based but attachment-friendly and warm manner.

Relationship Development Intervention with Children, Adolescents, and Adults by Steven E. Gutstein and Rachelle K. Sheely (Jessica Kingsley Publishers, 2002).

This book and the one that follows are the curricula for developing social skills. They are fantastic resources for schools and homes.

Relationship Development Intervention with Young Children by Steven E. Gutstein and Rachelle K. Sheely (Jessica Kingsley Publishers, 2002).

This book and the previous one are the curricula for developing social skills. They are fantastic resources for schools and homes.

Self-Calming Cards by Elizabeth Crary and Mits Katayama (Parenting Press, 2006).

This is a deck of cards that shows calming skills. Children aged 3–11 can pick out their favorite cards. Easy visuals show children what to do. The cards have Spanish or English words to match the pictures on the cards.

Skills Training for Children with Behavioral Problems (Revised Edition) by Michael Bloomquist (Guilford Press, 2006).

This is an excellent guide for parents and professionals who want tools, charts, and practical suggestions for reducing anger and anxiety, through changes in thinking and reward systems. It helps the whole family with better self-control and helpful thoughts.

Taking Charge of ADHD by Russell A Barkley (Guilford Press, 1995, revised 2005).

The author explains simply, but not superficially, what is going on with children with attention deficit hyperactivity disorder and what to do about it. Russell Barkley is not only a prolific writer and researcher, but he is a caring advocate for children and their families.

The Whole-Brain Child by Daniel Siegel and Tina Bryson (Bantam Books, 2012).

This book helps parents to coach the development of better emotional control. It is full of strategies that reflect Dan Siegel's ongoing contributions in helping families with attachment and emotional regulation.

Welcoming a New Brother or Sister Through Adoption by Arleta James (Jessica Kingsley Publishers, 2012).

This is a thorough, clear-headed look at adoption and the needs of all of the children in the family.

Zachery's New Home by Geraldine Blomquist and Paul Blomquist (Magination Press, 1991).

This is an all-time favorite with fostered or adopted children about beginning to trust after abuse.

Appendix A

COMMON QUESTIONS AND ANSWERS ON ATTACHING AND LIMITING

Question: *I have heard that babies and young children only bond or attach to their mothers, or to one parent at a time, for the first year of life.*

Answer: That is not true. When two parents are involved in the daily care of babies or young children, they both develop attachments to their little ones. In decades past, when it was typical for a mother to provide the care for the baby, some fathers only got involved after the first year of life. Now that it is typical for parents to share the care, both parents show strong attachments.

Question: *My child was adopted. I have heard it said that I need to show dominance, like in the animal world, in order to have my child respect me and see me as a leader.*

Answer: This is bad advice. It comes from some outdated information that applied dog training to people. It includes having children practice "sit" and "stay" like a dog, or following a strong leader, as in a wolf pack. These approaches have been debunked by research and common sense. People who used such approaches were well meaning, but misinformed. These approaches tended to frustrate children and damage real relationship-building for many children, although they helped some. They gained popularity in the 1980s when people were desperate for help with attachment problems. There was little professional help or advice for attachment disorders.

Question: *My child was sexually abused. Should I wait to touch her until she asks for touch? I am afraid of hurting her further with my affection.*

Answer: Children who were sexually abused need appropriate, affectionate touching, as we all do. Often I ask permission from children who are still guarded after sexual abuse, before I hold their hands, squeeze their shoulders gently, or rub their upper backs between their shoulder blades. I can demonstrate the touch on another person. When they see that it looks safe, then they will say, "Oh, that's OK." Children or teens who were sexually abused need lots of normal, appropriate touching to replace the toxic, sexualized touching that they experienced. When I work with children or teens who were sexually abused, I find it is not uncommon for them to turn to their parents at the end of the session, ready for a hug. Part of their healing is enjoying normal physical affection.

Question: *My adoption agency said to give my daughter information about her adoption as she asks for it. Is this correct? Recently I found a school assignment in which she describes missing her birth parents.*

Answer: I like to give information about adoption the way I would any important topic. I provide information and a context so that children do not get their information from the media or in a piecemeal manner. Because children do not have much abstract ability, they often have trouble putting their concerns or questions into a question format. I discuss adoption openly, giving information in stages, starting at about the age of three years old. Adoption is so dramatized in our society that I would prefer to give personally tailored information, with emotional support, at different stages. The first telling is at the age of 3–4 years old, when children learn that they started life inside their birthmothers. At the age of 6–8, many children realize that adoption has loss elements and will want to discuss this. During ages 9–10, children want more facts about their adoptions and their origins. Parents will need to help with this information. At ages 11–12 children try to understand their adoption story on a more abstract level. This continues through early adulthood. At this stage they need a "why" as well as the meaning of the facts from earlier ages. At ages 13–14 teens are trying to understand how they are like or unlike their birth relatives as well as their adoptive families. After that, keeping the topic open allows teens to ask when they want more information or need more discussion. Research shows that teens with open discussions about adoption have an easier time understanding who they are. They function better.[1]

Question: *Should I spank?*
Answer: I think that it is best to use negative consequences that exclude physical punishment. Spanking has downsides: teaching children not to hit others when they have just been hit, and worrying about spanking too hard. Teaching self-control is more reliable.

Question: *I have the chance to leave my four-year-old child for a month, for a once-in-a-lifetime trip. I am a stay-at-home parent. Will this hurt my child's attachment?*
Answer: Yes. At this stage of development, think in terms of a 3–5 day trip as the maximum time to leave your child. Your little one is also in a "once-in-a-lifetime" stage of development. Your absence will cause a grave loss.

Question: *I have been told that I need to sleep with my babies and children in order to have the best attachment possible. Is this necessary? I am tired.*
Answer: Enjoy your own bed. Co-sleeping is not necessary for secure attachments between you and your baby or child. If you want to share a bed, it is fine. It is not necessarily going to improve your attachment, though. And, if you are tired and grumpy, it probably is taking away from the quality of your attachment. Eating together, snuggling, sensitive parenting, and playing together are all more important.

Question: *I was told that children have formed their notions about attachment by the time they are 18 months to two years. They will not change much after that. Is this true?*
Answer: This is not true. This was a theory at one time. People thought that there was a "critical window." Actually, it is common for children over the age of two years old to develop secure attachments after rough starts, foster care, or orphanage care. They need a sensitive, attuned, and consistent parent to make the changes. Of course, attaching is more difficult after children come

---

1   Brodzinsky, D. and Schechter, M. (1990) *The Psychology of Adoption.* Oxford: Oxford University Press.

to families when they are older, or after backgrounds of neglect and trauma, but the odds are still positive ones.

Question: *My child was traumatized early in life. Will this interfere with attachment?*
Answer: Yes. It is likely that it will make attaching more difficult. That is why you will want to find therapy to address the impacts of trauma on your child. You will also do best to learn about and use specialized parenting. Children do so much better after therapy. My book, *Nurturing Adoptions: Creating Resilience after Trauma and Neglect*, listed in the Resources section, describes the symptoms of trauma at each childhood stage, as well as parenting that helps children at each stage. This is helpful whether or not your child was adopted. There is also a wonderful website for parents in the Resources—the Child Trauma Academy.

Question: *My child was abused by his mother. I am the step-mother. I am doing most of the parenting now, since we have custody. I notice that when I am harsher with my child, he actually obeys better. Should I use a harsher style, since it is the one that works best?*
Answer: No. Long term your children will show more behavior problems, and less empathy towards others. Your short-term benefit is not worth the long-term cost. Increase the structure and supervision of your child, instead. It is confusing for children when they have a nurturing parent instead of a harsh one. Their first reaction is to try to turn you into a familiar type of parent. Long term, we want them to drop their defenses, relating to a kind, sensitive parent.

Question: *My child does not look at me. I have been told to hold him, making him look at me. I am afraid that it might harm our attachment, but I am willing to try it if it would help him.*
Answer: This is well-intentioned, but outmoded information that is actually harmful to attachment in many cases. Encourage and reward eye contact. But, please do not coerce eye contact.

Question: *My child calls me names. I have tried ignoring it. Should I call him names back to see how he likes it?*
Answer: Please don't act like a misbehaving child. Please do require him to make amends through extra jobs, an earlier bedtime, or loss of another privilege.

Question: *My child looks like he has attention deficit disorder (ADD) and is hyperactive in situations that are unstructured. I do not think that he has ADD since he can watch television or play with his game console for hours. Why can he attend to TV when he cannot remember to turn in his homework or find matching shoes?*
Answer: Attention deficit disorder means that children have trouble not only paying attention, but shifting attention. It is actually harder for children with ADD to shift away from TV or computer games. Children with ADD have the most trouble getting "stuck" on computer games or TV. Other children shift away from computer or television with only mild or moderate effort.

It is also more difficult for children with ADD to remember what they are supposed to be attending to. So, while another child might be able to watch the clock while playing on their game console, getting ready to get off the game when necessary, this divided focus will be extremely challenging for children with ADD. Loud protests and late departures are normal for children with ADD when their game-playing is interrupted.

Question: *Are there things that I should avoid when I am parenting? I want a secure attachment, but was raised by alcoholic parents. I have a hard time knowing when I am in a danger zone.*
Answer: Please *avoid* all of the behaviors listed below. When tempted, note the reactions, which would make any parent cringe. I have detailed them in a negative manner, because it is much easier to recognize their harm.

- *Call your child names.* This will ensure that your bullying will cause your child to cringe around you, avoiding you. They will become skilled at lying and sneaking around you. Do not be surprised if they carry on your disrespect of them into a disrespect of others—making them vulnerable to bullying and being bullied.

- *Hit and slap your child when you are upset.* This will cause them to be frightened of you. They will wish for closeness with you and also wish for distance. Usually the distance wins out. They will either think that they are so irritating that they cause you to lash out, or that you are an out-of-control person. Neither is a compliment or a basis for healthy relationships.

- *Talk about the faults of their other parent, colluding with your child in your relationship problems.* Have the child take sides with you against the other parent. This will ensure that the child feels too much responsibility for your well-being and feels guilty and angry at sharing secrets with you.

- *Drink excessively or use drugs that alter behavior.* This will totally confuse your child, making them feel scared, nervous, and angry. They will feel the need to control you, and additionally think that it is their fault that you abuse substances. They will try, unsuccessfully, to think of strategies to keep you clean and sober. They will feel that they are not worth your staying sober.

- *Keep to a care schedule that follows your convenience.* Tell them to wait, and then wait longer when they are hungry, thirsty, and need to use the bathroom. Let them know that the adult's schedule takes priority and that they should suffer in silence. That will ensure that they will dislike you as well as feel shame over their bodily needs.

- *Laugh at your child's distress.* Act like their painful expressions are silly, and that they deserve to be mocked. This way they will feel ashamed of any weakness in themselves. They may grow up to use this attitude on others—including you.

The list looks overwhelming and negative. Yet, many parents struggle with these simple issues after experiencing poor models themselves. If you avoid the above list and try to follow the principles in this book, you will stay on a firm footing.

Question: *My child had his first depression in late primary school and then a serious depressive period in high school. He looks good, but I feel like he might need extra support before going to university.*

Answer: Having a gap year, or a year of taking college classes while staying at home, would be a great idea. Many teens struggle with their transition away from their parents, especially teens with a known vulnerability. Taking it in half-steps would be prudent.

Appendix B

BEHAVIORAL CHECKLIST FOR PATTERNS OF ATTACHMENT

I developed this checklist, giving people a way of looking at the behaviors between parents and children. While the checklist is made for use by professionals, it is valuable for parents as a reference. If you would like to see how you are doing, have a trusted, well-balanced friend, or a spouse, observe you with your child. Check off the behaviors that you and your child show over a 15-minute period of time. See how many check marks you have in each of the styles. Over time, try to have your pattern move more into the "secure" style.

Secure style indicators

❑ Child clings to parent when uncertain.

❑ Child references parent's face for cues about other people or the setting. She is reassured.

❑ Child follows parent around room with eyes, without being wary.

❑ Child smiles back at parent.

❑ Child initiates smile to parent.

❑ Child initiates or responds to little games and playful interactions with parent.

❑ Child prefers being within three feet (one meter) of parent rather than alone, while getting used to the observer or space.

❑ Child brings parent closer when playing.

❑ Child shows enhanced enjoyment when getting parent's attention.

❑ Child reaches towards parent, and then moves towards parent.

❑ Child anticipates that the parent will help when they are distressed or frustrated. They look at the parent, then anticipate parental involvement.

❑ Child looks to parent to share positive feelings.

❑ Child leans against parent and relaxes.

❑ Child looks to parent when confused—and then looks reassured.

❑ Child climbs onto parent's lap or overlaps parent (leans, rests, or sits on parent) when needing a break from stimulation.

❑ At a mis-step in play (poor-timing, conflict) or a tough transition, parent attempts a repair (an apology). The child accepts the repair.

❑ Child protests and becomes mildly upset when parent leaves room. Child calms quickly when parent comes back.

❑ Parent calms overexcited child with voice tones, distraction, or touch.

❑ Parent organizes child's time, providing structure in a calming voice.

❑ Parent touches child to guide, reassure, or to connect.

❑ Parent uses gaze to share delight.

❑ Parent's talk allows for pauses that child can fill.

❑ Parent allows child to introduce items into the play—then follows their lead.

❑ Parent matches or notes child's facial or body expressions.

❑ Parent interprets child's expressions indicating that they are thinking of the child's point of view.

❑ Parent distracts when child is frustrated.

❑ Parent prepares child for transitions.

❑ Parent's body and voice tones stay steady, but empathetic, when child is emotionally upset.

❑ At a mis-step in play (poor timing, conflict) or during a transition, parent attempts a repair (an apology or soothing explanation). The child does not accept it. The parent stays emotionally balanced.

❑ Parent guides child through transition, speaking about child's feelings if child is upset.

❑ Parent sets limits if play gets too unruly. Puts items away and introduces something else.

Insecure attachment indicators— preoccupied or dismissive parents

❑ Parent talks over child.

❑ Parent begins to play and then drifts off.

❑ Parent moves out of postures that allow child to nestle.

❑ Parent sits or stands so that child cannot easily scan their facial expressions or have body contact.

❑ Parent notices child's facial expressions but does not sustain interest in them.

❑ Parent talks about self and their point of view during play or transitions without trying to include the child's point of view.

❑ Child does not hold parent's attention, with parent discontinuing the play without signaling a transition.

❑ Parent argues with child over the play activity.

❑ Parent is impatient with child's anxiety when parent needs to leave or return to the room.

❑ Parent threatens child rather than giving limits (e.g. "You do that and you'll be sorry").

❑ Child looks at parent for play cues, but finds that parent is thinking about something else.

❑ Child asks repeatedly for needs or things, needing repetitions to get parent's attention.

❑ Child does not connect with parent's facial expressions except briefly, and then turns away.

Insecure attachment indicators— anxious or ambivalent child

❑ Parent makes statements like: "I don't know what you want. I don't know what to do."

❑ Parent spends a lot of time in tense silence.

❑ Parent makes anxious comments about child's stress during play or transition.

❑ Parent anxiously talks about self and their point of view during play or transitions without trying to include child's point of view.

❑ Parent announces the transition with too much advance warning, and conveys tension well before and after the transition.

❑ Parent apologizes to child for the normal structure rather than supporting structure, i.e. rules, times to leave, normal limits.

❑ Parent conveys anxiety to child with non-verbal cues and facial expressions. Sees anxiety in child and amplifies the anxiety.

Insecure style: anxious resistant or ambivalent

❑ Child looks at parent quickly and then looks away, showing some of parent's anxious expression.

❑ Child gets frustrated with a problem in play, but does not reach out to parent confidently. May say, "You probably won't help me with this." Complains about the quality of parent's help after parent helps.

❑ Child clings to parent, but does not settle or regulate better with body contact.

❑ Child climbs parent's body roughly, with parent wincing, and with no change in child's expression in relation to parent's non-verbal cues.

❑ Child drums feet against parent when being held.

❑ Child asks for items, but then abandons them.

❑ Child discontinues gaze with parent in order to better self-regulate.

❑ Child continues to signal distress long after the transition (whines, complains, bats at parent).

Insecure style: avoidant

❑ Child sits outside of social distance (about five feet or 1.5 meters) from parent throughout observation.

❑ Child sits with back to parent.

❑ Child stiffens when touched by parent.

❑ Child gets frustrated with a problem in play, but does not reach out to parent confidently. May say, "You probably won't help me with this."

❑ Child grabs toys away from parent during play.

❑ Child looks at parent quickly, and then looks away.

❑ Parent does not hold child's attention, with child moving on before parent can respond.

❑ Parent does not share time or activity with child (e.g. plays with building activity by building their own structure).

❑ Parent tells child that they are not playing right (e.g. "Are you doing this right?").

❑ Parent shrugs when child ignores, excludes, or resists parental interaction.

❑ Child persists with negative behaviors that are not allowed.

❑ Parent is critical or sarcastic with child.

Disorganized/disoriented style

❑ Parent gives up on limits and begins to ignore behaviors (e.g. lets child use markers after asking child to move to table, or, child stands on sofa when parent requests that they sit).

❑ Parent acts like they cannot set limits or please their child. Uses a helpless, beseeching manner with other adults around.

❑ Parent comments positively about child's misbehavior.

❑ Parent comments in defeated manner about their role in the failure of the limit-setting. Parent may become tearful.

❑ Parent makes negative attributions of child in regards to limit-setting (e.g. "She's just like my sister, the drug-addict").

❑ Parent describes psychologically painful losses or trauma while with child, forgetting impact on child.

❑ Parent has child take charge. Parent moves to play the part of the child rather than just allowing child to lead.

❑ Parent does not reference the effect that the behavior above has on child.

❑ Child uses avoidance strategies (covering ears, shouting, etc.) if parent describes stressful life events.

❑ Child gets angry at parent as parent describes stressful life events.

❑ Child comforts parent when parent describes other psychologically stressful life events in the observation.

❑ Child asks for parent and then lies on floor, face averted from parent or face down.

❑ Parent does not successfully move child through transition, and abandons the goals (e.g. gives up on teeth brushing, coat on or off, dinner at the table, hand-washing, and tasks that will cause frustration).

❑ Parent describes child as "He's just like that/He was always that way." Does not have a theory of mind.

❑ Child watches parent warily.

❑ Child makes punitively controlling comments to parent.

❑ Child makes controlling comments to parent, as in taking care of parent.

❑ Child warns others not to hurt or upset parent.

❑ Child freezes when parent comes close.

❑ Child freezes when parent's partner comes close.

❑ Child becomes still-faced (blank expression) when parent holds them or snuggles.

❑ Child covers genitals when caregiver comes close.

❑ Child covers genitals when caregiver's partner comes close.

❑ Child covers face when caregiver's partner comes close.

❑ Child covers face when caregiver comes close.

❑ Child wails and becomes disorganized when parent leaves room. Child is aggressive to parent when parent comes back.

❑ Child runs around room in a frenzied manner. Gets less organized when closest to parent.

❑ Child hits parent, throws things at parent, slams items on parent's hands. (Child follows-up with a look of triumph or panic.)

❑ Child runs to parent, veers away, and then cries.

❑ Child avoids parent gaze, looking at parent covertly. (This does not include Asian or Native American children.)

❑ Child looks dazed, moves in slow motion.

❑ Child freezes when approaching parent.

❑ Child expresses anger in observation much more than is typical of age.

❑ Parent scares child. Child looks scared. Parent laughs.

❑ Parent does the same behavior as above, repeating the overwhelming play.

❑ Child makes large motor movement to "scatter" parent away.

❑ With the above, parent does not attempt to attribute a meaning.

❑ Parent repeatedly moves out of social distance from child.

❑ Parent attempts to bring up subjects of interest—not finding the interaction with child interesting enough.

❑ Parent brings up traumatic material into play or conversation.

❑ Parent does the above, and encourages child's support.

❑ Parent makes negative attributions about child.

❑ At a mis-step in play (poor timing, conflict), parent attempts a repair. Child does not accept the repair. Parent responds in a peer manner, "Be like that."

❑ Parent repeatedly overstimulates child, even positively.

❑ Parents uses too frightening a voice in play, notes that the child is frightened, but then does not self-correct.

❑ Parent brings up trauma themes in play.

❑ Parent dissociates during observation.

❑ Parent lifts lips and shows teeth in play. Child is frightened. Parent laughs.

❑ Parent and child play babies. Parent is baby repeatedly.

❑ Parent asks child to come close, and then moves further away.

These are patterns of behavior. Parents who are finding items in the disorganized category are encouraged to engage in therapy. If they find that the check-marks are beside "anxious, avoidant, and disorganized parent," it is a wonderful time to make changes in parenting.

Appendix C

CHORES BY AGE

Ages 2–3 years

Picks up toys and books. This may start with the parents guiding hands.

Pulls up comforter on bed.

Dusts. Put an old sock or mitten on child's hand for dusting.

Puts dirty laundry in laundry basket.

Takes own socks, shirts, and pants from clean laundry pile.

Helps mop up spills.

Washes hands with help.

Ages 4–5 years

Helps set the table.

Wipes off counter after teeth brushing.

Brushes teeth. (Parents will brush teeth again and will floss.)

Puts dirty dishes in the dishwasher.

Dusts (simple surfaces).

Brings small garbage cans from around the house for emptying.

Picks up toys and books in their own room and in common spaces.

Sorts clothes from laundry pile.

Folds face cloths or hand towels.

Puts food out for pets, with supervision to be sure that this is done.

Carries light grocery bags into the house.

Puts away the clean silverware.

Washes hands after toileting and before eating, with some reminding.

Ages 6–8 years

All of the above plus:

Puts away clean clothes, learns to fold clothes.

Sorts recycling.

Takes recycling and small bags of garbage to outside can or bin.

Takes dirty sheets off bed and helps to put on clean bedding.

Vacuums.

Cleans sinks.

Wipes up spills.

Puts out food and water for pets—with overseeing.

Sweeps decks or walkway.

Brushes teeth, bathes or showers every other day, and washes hands after toileting and before eating.

Ages 9–12 years

All of the above plus:

Changes sheets and makes bed, even if more complex than comforter.

Cleans own room.

Loads and unloads dishwasher, or washes, dries, and puts away dishes. May need help with pots and pans earlier in the age range.

Cleans bathroom.

Gets clothes in and out of washing machine.

Helps with yard work—raking leaves, weeding, and finally operating the lawn mower or lawn tools by the end of the age range.

Vacuums out the car.

Picks up after the dog and cleans out the cat box.

Showers/bathes, and shampoos own hair, but needs reminding.

Age 13 years and up

All of the above plus:

Can arrange furniture.

Learns to clean furniture and floors.

Uses household appliances.

Learns and can use first aid.

Volunteers some help in the community.

Uses an organizational system for school papers.

Makes medical appointments by 18 years old, with overseeing.

Takes care of a pet.

Showers/bathes daily without supervision or reminding.

COMMUNICATING WITH HIGHLY STRESSED CHILDREN AND ADULTS

Stress is a necessary part of life. Our bodies respond to stress by producing a burst of stress hormones. The hormones give us the energy and urge to mobilize, to solve problems, and to respond physically to a stressor. Examples of stress hormones that work to our benefit are: studying hard for exams, providing first aid to people in emergencies, or fixing homes and property after a bad storm. When stress is non-stop, we actually find that it damages us. It impacts our memories, our ability to understand complicated information, our ability to organize, and our ability to put what we need into words. Because of the impact of stress, people often find it difficult to communicate with stressed family members. The following is a guide to communication with stressed people. It is applicable for both children and adults.

Issues and responses
1. Feelings are not stable
RESPONSES:

- *Keep yourself centered and stable.* You need to stay healthy in attitude and body.

- *Do not limit your commitment and love, but do limit your exposure to the amount of time or stress that you are able to handle.* "I am not completely available; I am completely committed."

- *Share the wealth.* Include other stable adults in supporting this person. (Watch out for jealous reactions if your family member says something like, "Ms. X helped me so much in just an afternoon.")

- *Maintain your self-interest.* Have interests and activities beyond the sphere of your loved one's stress. Their stress does not dictate your ability to enjoy your life.

- *Help to provide perspective.* For older children, teens, and adults, help to explore alternatives. This sounds like, "I wonder if we could explore, just for a moment, a possible compromise or alternative." This works better than "I think that you are over-reacting."

- *Show compassion for their wounding, their pain, when they get stuck in an "all or nothing" position.* Often people become stuck in a position because it mirrors their pain or loss. Acknowledge the pain, but see if they are able to move into more helpful ways of thinking.

- *Give ample attention when things are going relatively well.* Share the pleasure of spending time with them when things are stable. This encourages more stability, since they get attention when steady.

- *Give the stressed person the sense that "you are holding them in your mind."* Stress includes the distortion that there is no one to count on, no one who really understands, or who truly cares. Counteract this with comments like, "I noticed you. I was thinking about you. I am here for you."

- *Model and practice calming techniques like deep breathing, meditating, praying, singing, listening to music, walking, exercising, etc.*

2. Brain changes occur, making it difficult to remember things or to organize life. Brain changes may include: impulsivity, seeing details and missing the big picture, problems organizing, difficulty with complexity, inability to screen out noise, and limits on how much information the brain is able to process.
RESPONSES:
Number events. For example, in speaking to children we might say, "There are three things that we do to finish the task.

    1 is _____

    2 is _____

3 is _____."

"What is number 1?" the child responds.

The parent says, "Great, let's start."

In speaking to an adult we would say, "There are three things to do in the next 15 minutes before we leave. First, I want you to get the folder for the meeting. Second, I want us both to get coats and keys. Third, I will put the dog in. Will you please get the papers for the meeting now?"

Executive functioning is impaired to some degree in most people who are highly stressed. Initiating is part of executive functioning. When to start becomes a moving target—and a tremendous source of frustration for everyone. Set a time for starting. "What will be the time to do X?" Let the person set the time if at all possible.

- *Use raised fingers to help with counting.* For example, there are four things that we need to do in the morning before school. Put up four fingers. Name the items. Then put up number one, saying, "Start." The visual cues help.

- *List daily schedules.* Use visuals for small children. Put in time for free time or choice.

- *Put in time on the daily schedule for talking or problem-solving.* Teach the brain to defer worry and to schedule problem-solving.

- *Speak simply.* Use shorter sentences. Speak more slowly. Put the subject and verb in that order. Shared stress often causes the caregiver or family member to talk too much. Do not become the irritating wallpaper for an overwhelmed person.

- *Maintain a predictable and organized home.* Limit commotion in the home. Reduce variables, like overnight guests, transitions, traveling, changing daily schedules.

- *Give breaks in the day for exercise or goofing off.* The stressed person has more need to "run off" or "work off" high stress. Some need naps. Provide time for these breaks.

3. The person ignores or forgets requests that are given in a normal tone with a normal amount of emotion.
RESPONSES:

- *Set limits, enforce limits, but do it calmly. Resist adding your emotion to their organizational problems.* Big emotional displays may work in the short term to get the attention of the anxious person, but over time create even more anxiety in the home and relationship.

- *Create written memos as reminders.* Computer-based reminders or cell phone reminders work well.

- *Normalize their experience.* Important message are: "Right now you seem stressed. It's normal for any of us under stress to forget or tune out. I don't want to nag you. If there's something important, how should we handle reminders?" See if the person has ideas. If not, suggest two. Let the person choose one. A teen asked if they could create a checklist. Another teen put a reminder on his cell phone calendar.

- *Notice and comment on times that the person remembers.* Help them to see their increasing mastery of daily demands.

4. Stress makes the person harder to connect with.
RESPONSES:
Create times for connection.

- *Meals are an excellent time to connect.* Talk about favorite foods, recipes, and tastes. It helps the person to enjoy life.

- *Consider getting a dog if you struggle to find things in common.* You can always talk about the dog. Also, dogs are a good antidote for low mood.

- *Increase positive looping—back-and-forth conversations that are completely positive.*

- *Make zones of time that are completely positive.* For example, homework, jobs, and chores are off-limits during mealtimes or in the car.

- *Touch the person positively if they permit this.*

- *Value the person's friends, making them welcome.*

- *Lie down with the person when talking, if this is appropriate for the age, sex, and relationship.* Nest. It is comfortable to speak when both are stretched out on the bed, on the couch or an easy chair.

- *Have times when you are sitting and easily available* (not tensely lurking). TV computer, or cell phone texting does not signal that you are "available."

- *Look for topics that are common to you and the stressed person.* This might be singers, paintball, the pyramids and ancient peoples, etc.

- *Include a mix of ideas for family projects.* Elicit the stressed person's ideas and be sure to incorporate them. (Often there is a sour, first reaction, followed by positive involvement.)

- *Elicit the person's world view.* Do not argue with it, but show curiosity and interest in how they came to that point of view. Talking aloud will help the person examine their own thinking.

- *When the stressed person withdraws, do not withdraw in turn.* You can conclude: "It seems that you are done talking right now. I hope that we can talk again some time."

- *Do not pretend to connect when you are not able to connect with the person.* Work at connecting, but avoid being artificially "happy-acting." It feels false and awkward.

5. Person loses a sense of hope or perspective
RESPONSES:

- *Maintain hope.* If you are not on a positive course, hold fast to the notion that you will find resources that will give you hope.

- *Qualify negativity while extending empathy.* "It seems that you have kind of given up right now. I haven't. However, I can accept that things seem bleak right now. I'm so sorry."

- *Do not exaggerate the differences between you and the stressed person by saying,* "I do X and therefore [do so much better than you]." The person is already feeling hopeless. It is easier to say: "It seems that you feel that nothing will help right now. Most of us go through times like that." Later, you can ask if the person wants some ideas about how things could change. Or, "Let me know if you want to talk about this further."

- *Help the person generate their own ideas and perspectives when in relationship dilemmas.* Do not tell the person what to do. Do allow them the chance to discuss pros and cons.

6. Person lacks or has difficulty with self-skills. Self-skills are: putting things into perspective, being flexible, calming, generating strategies or plans, looking at things through another's perspective without losing their own point of view or interest.
RESPONSES:

- *Model self-skills.*

- *Teach self-skills* to younger children and teens/adults who are open to them.

- *Enrol children, teens, and adults in skills groups and/or obtain individual therapy.*

- *Help the person calm with you,* using your well-regulated brain to teach them the pattern of calming.

- *Attune, with empathy, to the stressed person.* Get on the same wavelength. Over time, people learn how to keep up their end of the relationship.

- *Give stressed people the chance to use their perspective talking with you or others.* Help them to generate ideas for others.

- *Make plans and develop strategies for difficult or stressful situations.*

After stressful experiences, people have the task of putting together a life story that incorporates all of their life events. Highly stressed events or traumatic events are, by definition, hard to incorporate. Do get professional help.

The rewards for all are evident as stressed people begin to hope, notice areas of mastery, and see their progress. They are more open to relationships and new experiences. They show increased curiosity about life, increased interest in daily events, and increased hope for a positive future that they will help to shape.

ADDITIONAL REFERENCES

Aguilar, B., Sroufe, L.A., Egeland, B., and Carlson, E. (2000) "Distinguishing the early-onset/persistent and adolescence-onset antisocial behavior types: From birth to 16 years." *Development and Psychopathology* 12: 109–132.

Arvidson, J., Kinniburgh, K., Howard, K., Spinazzola, J., *et al.* (2011) "Treatment Of Complex Trauma In Young Children: Developmental And Cultural Considerations In Application Of The ARC Intervention Model." *Journal of Child and Adolescent Trauma* 4: 34–51.

Bates, B. and Dozier, M. (2002) "The importance of maternal state of mind regarding attachment and infant age at placement to foster mothers' representations of their foster infants." *Infant Mental Health Journal* 23(4): 417–431.

Belsky, J. and Fearon, R.M. (2002) "Early attachment security, subsequent maternal sensitivity, and later child development: Does continuity in development depend upon continuity of caregiving?" *Attachment and Human Development* 4(2): 361–387.

Bowlby, J. (1983). *Attachment and Loss, Vol. 1: Attachment.* New York: Basic Books.

Cox, A. (2008) *No Mind Left Behind: Understanding and Fostering Executive Control.* New York: Perigee Press.

Dawson, P., and Guare, R. (2010) *Executive Skills in Children and Adolescents.* New York: Guilford Press.

Dozier, M., Pelosoa, E., Lewis, E., Laurenceaua, J., and Levine, S. (2008) "Effects of an attachment-based intervention on the cortisol production of infants and toddlers in foster care." *Development and Psychopathology* 20: 845–859.

Egeland, B., Carlson, E., and Sroufe, L.A. (1993) "Resilience as Process." *Development and Psychopathology* 5: 517–528.

Fisher, P.A. *et al.* (2011) "Mitigating HPA Axis Dysregulation Associated with Placement Changes in Foster Care." *Psychoneuroendocrinology* 36(4): 531–539.

Foa, E., Keane, T., Friedman, M., and Cohen, J. (eds) (2009) *Effective Treatments for PTSD* (2nd ed.). New York: Guilford Press.

Gray, D. (2012a) *Nurturing Adoptions: Creating Resilience after Trauma and Neglect.* London: Jessica Kingsley Publishers.

Gray, D. (2012b) *Attaching in Adoption: Practical Tools for Today's Parents.* London: Jessica Kingsley Publishers.

Gunnar, M. and Cheatham, C. (2003) "Stress and the Developing Brain." *Infant Mental Health Journal* 24(3): 195–2011.

Hughes, D. (2007) *Attachment-Focused Family Therapy.* New York: Norton Press.

Hughes, D. (2009) *Attachment-Focused Parenting.* New York: Norton Press.

Leve, L.D., Fisher, P.A., and Chamberlain, P. (2009) "Multidimensional Treatment Foster Care as a preventative intervention to promote resiliency among youth in the child welfare system." *Journal of Personality* 77: 1869–1902.

Lewis, E.E., Dozier, M., Ackerman, J., and Sepulveda-Kozakowski, S. (2007) "The effect of placement instability on adopted children's inhibitory control abilities and oppositional behavior." *Development and Psychology* 43: 1415–1427.

Lieberman, A., and Van Horn, P. (2008) *Psychotherapy with Infants and Young Children.* New York: Guilford Press.

Lyons-Ruth, K., Jacobvitz, D. (2008) "Chapter 28: Attachment Disorganization." In J. Cassidy and P. Shaver (eds) *Handbook of Attachment*, p.8. New York: Guilford Press.

Pears, K.C., Kim, J.K., and Fisher, P. (2008) "Psychosocial and cognitive functioning of children with specific profiles of maltreatment." *Child Abuse and Neglect* 32: 958–971.

Schore, A. (2003) *Affect Dysregulation*, p.250. New York: Norton Press.

Solomon, J., and George, C. (eds) (1999) *Attachment Disorganization.* New York: Guilford Press.

Solomon, M., and Siegel, D. (eds) (2003) *Healing Trauma: Attachment, Mind, Body and Brain.* New York: Norton Press.

Sroufe, L.A. (1995) *Emotional Development.* Cambridge: Cambridge University Press.

Sroufe, L.A. (1997) "Psychopathology as outcome of development." *Development and Psychopathology* 9: 251–268.

Waters, V. (1999) Chapter 10: "Explaining Disorganised Attachment." In J. Solomon and C. George (eds) *Attachment Disorganization*, pp.265–285. New York: Guilford Press.

INDEX